# *The Life History*
## of
# Robert Jared Dickson

# The Life History
## of
# Robert Jared Dickson

Top row: Earl, Henry, Jared, Newell, and John; Bottom row: Katie, Dad (William), Aunt Emma (stepmother), and Thelma

# CHILDHOOD

I was born May 31, 1921 in Kane, Bighorn County, Wyoming. My father was William Henderson Dickson and my mother was Edna Seviah Despain. I was the seventh child of a family of seven, having four brothers: Joseph Henry, Newell Despain, William Earl and John H. and two sisters: Edna Catherine (Katie) and Thelma.

My parents were pioneers of the Big Horn Basin. They were sent to settle and colonize the Cowley area by direction from The Church of Jesus Christ of Latter-day Saints headquarters in 1990. My dad was mostly a dirt farmer by occupation but was also known as a stockman and a very talented sheepshearer. He taught his family how to work and play and most of all to live the gospel standards.

We moved to Cowley when I was three years old and lived in a log cabin on a 120-acre farm. My dad and older brothers moved a large house onto the property the next year and we lived there until it burned in 1930. We had moved part of the old log house out a short distance and used it for a blacksmith shop.

Picture: Thelma, John, Jared, three-years-old

I was close to three years old before I started remembering things. However, I do remember a few things prior to that; like knowing where there was a warm place in the wood box next to the kitchen stove or learning I was too big to use the pot and having to go outside to use the toilet. I can remember Henry holding me in his arms for this operation when the snow was on the ground.

Henry has always been a second dad to me. Whatever he did or said had the same authority as if Dad was saying it. He was always there to help or stick up for me. He was a real friend all of my life. I learned a lot from Henry because of his integrity and his devotion to the truth and serving the Lord.

When I was four years old, all of us children got scarlet fever and were quarantined in the old house. After our family recovered from the disease, our neighbors, the Eyres, came down with it. Mama spent a lot of time tending to their needs and it was while doing this compassionate service that she contracted pneumonia.

Mama was very ill and quite a few of the family and neighbors had gathered knowing that her time was at hand. She called me to her bedside and made me promise to be a good boy. I had no idea what death was and could not understand why everyone was crying. I slipped out of the house and went out along the canal bank where I knew there was a turkey nest in the tall weeds. I was looking for more nests when our neighbor Sister Hope Eyre came looking for me and to tell me mama had passed away. As we walked along toward the house I heard this beautiful singing. I asked Sister Eyre what it was and she said, "No one is singing; everyone is crying." My dad told me later that what I heard was a celestial choir that had come to take mama home. It made such a vivid impression on me that as I write this experience eighty years later, I remember that occasion as if it were yesterday. I truly experienced a heavenly manifestation.

Mama died on May 24, 1926. She passed away just six days before my fifth birthday. My sister Katie was seventeen years old at this time and was left with the formidable task of taking over mamma's duties of raising a young family. With everyone's cooperation and the help of the Lord our family has always stayed close.

I was too young to realize just how bad things were, but Dad went through a great deal of trials the next few years. It probably started with Momma's death, but we saw him nearly blinded when some hot lead exploded in his face and the house burned. He was nearly crushed to death under the car and spent a long time in the hospital. The nation faced the greatest depression ever recorded. We had no money, but we had livestock and had a good garden, and with hard work and careful planning we were well fed and survived fine.

One day my dad borrowed a car from Elmer Eyre, because he had to give a church talk in Byron. But he got in the wrong car. The police arrested him in church. The car he used had government property in it because it was used to carry mail from the carbon plant. There was a big fuss about it, but people were on his side and no prosecution was made.

I started school at age six. It was never difficult for me as long as I studied and prepared, but it was easy to be distracted by sports and other fun things. I could have been at the top of the class if I had chosen to be. One of my teachers told my dad that and he kept me in line most of the time. I played football and basketball. I like to wrestle and box. I was never a great star in anything, but I didn't take a back seat to anyone when it came to horseback riding and ice skating.

The outhouse didn't have any windows and was way out back of the school house. We couldn't believe that people would actually put an outhouse inside the house. One day my brother John heard a big noise and wanted to go see what the noise was. He said, "You wouldn't believe what people were doing in that room. They would pull on the chain to flush the toilet and the water reservoir above the toilet would make a big noise. If you were standing too close, you would get wet.

Picture of Third Grade Class

Top row: Wyoming Hinckley (teacher); Middle row: Mary Diaz, Marjorie Eyre, Hermina Miller, Irene Lytheo, Eva Lou Marchant, Mary Mendosa, Betty Dalton, Anna Olson, Laura Lee Greg, Edna Tucker, and Dorothy Eyre; Bottom row: Huff Welch, Ray Harston, Elton Anderson, Dudley Godfrey, Heber Robb, Adolf Mendosa, Mariann

Anderson, Leo Baird, Norman March, Cal Harvey, Jared Dickson, Fred Smith

Aunt Emma came to our home the year I was seven. It wasn't easy for her. We went through some real trials, but she was always true and faithful and did her share and then some. She was a real companion for Dad. She showed her real mettle and veracity at the time the house burned. It seemed a lot of the times she showed favoritism towards John when he could do nothing wrong and I could do nothing right. After reflecting on this, I can agree that she was not always wrong.

Our first family vehicle was a 1928 Chevy. It had a big knob on it, four doors and a back seat. Dad drove it. He tried to teach Emma to drive at a park in Lovell. Dad would crank the car to start it and then get out of the way. When the car jumped onto the sidewalk and into a store, Emma decided she was done learning to drive. She did drive the car one time to town, very slowly. She said, "Oh, that darn pig followed me all the way to town."

The year I was eight, I was baptized in the canal by Elmer Eyre. Dorothy, his daughter, was baptized at the same time. The year I was nine-years-old I spent the summer with Granddad herding sheep up above Pryor Mountain. It took us four days to trail the sheep from the farm up to the summer range. At the point of the mountain, Grandad sent me back to the farm to get the hobbles and nose-bags for the horses. It was thirty-miles, which I rode in one day and returned the next day to catch up to the herd. They were ten miles farther up the trail from where I left them. I was really glad to reach the camp and have thought later that it was quite an undertaking for a nine-year-old. Herding sheep was an adventure; getting up early to fix breakfast and be ready to leave the camp at daylight. We would herd the sheep to a different part of the range each day and keep them from getting scattered. Around noon, we would drive them down to Sage Creek for water and there they would lie down for a couple of hours. During this time, we would eat lunch and usually take a nap. The sheep would feed in the late afternoon and just before dark we would have them back on the bed grounds. We had a lot of time to talk, dig sego lilies and watch for coyotes and bears. It was a great learning experience for me and I will never forget it.

As a youth, a typical summer day on the farm would seem to follow a certain routine. It would start early in the morning when Dad and Henry would get up early to tend to the irrigation. Newell would water and feed the horses. Earl, John and I would do the milking. Before I learned to milk a cow I would feed the chickens and pigs and other necessary chores before breakfast. Before meals, we would always kneel to pray and Dad would call on one of us to lead the prayer. If Dad wasn't here Katie or Henry would rule in his stead. At the table, we would discuss the important things that needed to be done and assignments were made. After breakfast, the real work day would begin. Henry would take one team and start mowing hay. Newell would take another team and start raking the hay that was cut the day before. Earl was extremely good on the best cultivator. The girls took care of the household chores. John and I took the cows and herded them on the ditch banks and in the washes and draws.

For any breakdowns in assignments or machinery, Henry would always be the first to notify us and correct the situation. The evening meal was always started with a word of prayer. After supper, the irrigation was adjusted for the night and last minute chores were secured. Dad and Henry would always make sure we were all saying our individual prayers.

Because it was the time of the great depression and a large family that needed support, Henry had to leave school and help on the farm to make ends meet. He never completed his high school education.

Around 1935 we bought the Ed Johnson place that quartered on our farm. That added another one hundred and sixty acres and it was called Henry's farm. I am not sure who held the title but we all worked on it.

One fun summer Henry had just acquired the new farm and was starting a new family with his pretty new wife, Geneva, but they had no place to live. Henry and Geneva, our sister Katie and her husband Kurt Karlinsey and I took a team of horses and went up to the Pryor mountains for a week and got enough logs for Henry to build his house. It was a fun camping trip. On the way home I stopped at the Frying Pan Hole on Crooked Creek and caught a mess of fish. I later took Henry there for a fun outing. That is where I concocted the yarn about the fish and frying pan with which I have entertained my friends and scouts for many years. A more detailed account is found in my personal journal.

Jared in front of Henry and Geneva's first house

EXCERPT FROM JARED DICKSON'S JOURNAL:

One day I wanted to go fishing and brought my fry pan with me so I could cook up a few fish. I tied a line on a big willow branch and put a grasshopper on the end of the line. I could see a huge fish and the fish grabbed for the grasshopper. The fish was too big to lift out with the line, so I jumped in the creek to get him. I stumbled on some slick rocks, but got the big fish to a sandy spot. I wanted to keep fishing so I tied the fry pan to the end of the fish's tail and put the fish under some brush. When I went back to the fry pan, fish and pan were gone. Did a coyote get it? A year later when I went back to the same hole, there was that big fish. I knew it was the same because it still had the fry pan tied to its tail. There were twenty little fish, and each had a fry pan attached to their tail.

The day Henry and I went to Crooked Creek there was no trail and at places we had to scale down small ledges. It was difficult for Henry because a few days before he had accidently shot himself in the right hand and was not able to use it. We built a fire and cooked the fish. It was always fun to be with Henry.

Jared, John, and Bart Dickson

I guess I lived a pretty normal life as a farm boy. I was very close to my brother John, and we shared many happy experiences. We probably did about everything that could be done on a farm and probably a lot of things we shouldn't have. We still laugh about the time the dogs chased a cat up a high corner post on the corral. When the cat got to the top, it never stopped. The cat jumped four feet higher than the post, fell back to the ground, and had to climb it again, more cautiously. Another time John was riding "Old Stubby" across the canal when the horse decided to lie down in the middle of the stream. Besides the farm work, we had to do things like putting up hay, thinning beets and irrigating. We still found time to build flippers (slingshots) and became crack shots with them. We killed a lot of sparrows and had a lot of meals with rabbits we shot with our flippers. We also found the time to draw out prairie dogs and ground owls. One time we told Walter Robb he could twist an owl's head off by walking around it. He walked around one for half an hour as it sat on a bush and watched him. He never did see the owl's head follow him to a certain position and quickly turn its head back to the original point so fast it could not be detected and appeared to be in constant rotation.

Two of the animals I became very attached to were Old Tip and Lightfoot. Old Tip was a border collie. Perhaps not purebred, but he had all the intelligent characteristics. He was mostly black but had a small white star on his forehead and another small patch of white on his chest. The last four inches of his tail was white. He had brown eyebrows and his ears stood nearly erect; only the tops dropped over a little. We raised him from a puppy and as John and I were quite young, the three of us grew up together. As far as I was concerned, he was one of the family. Old Tip was a well- trained farm dog. He saved us a lot of steps while herding sheep and cows. Sometimes just to shout his name would put the stock in line. He could catch baby chickens without hurting them or he could take on a mean horse and soon have him running. Old Tip was a real friend when it came to hunting and swimming. He loved to swim and would often wade in the ditch or swim in the canal just to cool off.

We would often tell this concocted story of how smart he was as a hunting dog. He had his own special bed in the grass under a willow tree that grew on the ditch bank near our front door. If we picked up the shovel to go irrigate or a hoe to work in the field or garden when we left the house, he would remain asleep and undisturbed. If we picked up a gun, he was up and all over you; ready to go. If you picked up the shotgun, he would ignore all other game and would hunt only ducks, pheasant and sage hens. But, if you picked up the .22, he ignored the birds and would hunt only rabbits and prairie dogs. If you picked up your fishing pole, he would immediately run to the garden and start digging worms.

## Picture of Old Rip (the son of Old Tip)

We had a small band of sheep on the farm that we would brand and send them with other small herds to make up a large herd for a permit to graze on the Bighorn Mountains. After lambing, and they were sheared. It was a sad day for John and me as my dad told the sheep man he could borrow Old Tip to trail to the mountains. Dad said, "Take care of him. He is just like one of the family." Mr. Jolley, the sheep man, responded, "Yeah, which one?" Dad ignored the sarcastic remark and we saw him put the dog in his truck and drive away.

A couple of weeks later Mr. Jolley came to the house to collect for the herd bill, and, of course, our concern was *where is the dog?* He said, "Oh we got through with him and sent him home. We fired a few shots at him and the last we saw, he was headed down the mountain."

The mountain pasture was about 50 miles from home and the route to get there was mostly through the Wyoming Badlands with two rivers to cross. A stray dog was always something for the ranchers to shoot at. We thought his chances of getting home were nil to none.

It was noon time and we had just eaten dinner, and, as usual, we had a couple of hours of rest before we went back to the fields. John and I were so distraught about the Old Tip. We got away from the house and that awful sheep man. We were sitting in the old car just waiting for the time to pass. John said we should pray for Old Tip instead of crying about it. Not five minutes later we saw in the distance a black dog coming up the road, but we didn't recognize him until he was within fifty yards of us. His tail was dragging and he had lost a lot of weight. He walked with very sore feet. We ran to meet him, and as we picked him up, we were both crying and hugging each other and the dog. After feeding him, he drank a half gallon of milk and seemed content to find his usual bed under the shade tree on the ditch bank where he lay for two days. It would be very interesting to know of his incredible journey to get back home. He was a real friend, and I hope to see him again in the resurrection.

Old Lightfoot was John's pony and was very valuable for transportation and hunting. You could lay your rifle across his back and fire at a deer using him for a dead rest. He was very spirited and when you climbed on him, he would immediately take off on a dead run. At the same time you could put a child on him and he would just walk until he had enough and then despite the child's efforts to keep him going, he would head for the barn.

Probably my first real responsibility on the farm was herding cows. John and I did it together until he got big enough to handle a team and irrigate. Then herding cows was my job to see that they were kept on grass along the ditch banks and washes. My favorite place to go was up along the canal. There was always good feed and lots of rabbits. I would see that they were always home in time for chores and were not abused to the point it harmed the milk production. When I was big enough to drive a team, pitch hay, etc., the cows were put in a fenced pasture and I worked the farm. A very choice part of my life was over.

I was twelve years old when we got our first tractor and slowly the horse teams were replaced, although Old Kit and Clabe remained until the farm was sold. I learned at an early age to handle a team and spent many hours working in the fields. With the advent of the tractors, a lot more work could be done in less time. I had a lot of responsibility as I got older. The years that I was sixteen to eighteen, I was left at home to put in the crops as Dad and all my brothers left to shear sheep at that time of the year. I usually had a hired man, Kurt Karlinsey, to help me. Aunt Emma, my stepmother, was invaluable in helping me plan a schedule in getting the work done.

My brothers would live with the family they were shearing sheep for. My brother, John, was big and could shear sheep with the best of them. After they had put all the sheep in the pens, the Sheepherder's Australian shepherd dog came by and John sheared the dog as well. The Sheepherder was furious and swung at John. John took him down and sheared off his beard and long hair. The rancher said he would have like to have done it himself.

Eight grade class. Mary Alice's dad, Charles Marchant, was the teacher. Front row: Leo Baird, Jared Dickson, Fred Smith. Second row: Anna Olson, Bernice Tucker, Betty Dalton, Marda Partrige, Esther Lewis, Evalou Marchant (daughter of teacher), Edna Tucker, Dorothy Eyre. Third row: Heber Robb, Elton Anderson, Dudley Godfrey, Cal Harvey

Life was really getting fun. The next year Dad bought me a .22 rifle that gave me a lot of enjoyment when I could afford the shells. I had learned to swim and could ride like the wind on Old Lightfoot. In the summertime, it was a daily occurrence to use the old swimming hole in the canal. Our neighbors, Neil, Lloyd and Jay Partridge, Carlyle and Rex Eyre, were usually there and we had a ball. We swam Old Lightfoot through the hole and he loved it. One of the Stevens kids brought their horse, Old Croppy, and John rode him through the hole. When he got to the deep part, the horse couldn't swim and so he disappeared under the swift water. John held onto the reins and Old Croppy reappeared about 100 feet downstream at the shallow end. Old Croppy let out a big groan and blew water out of both nostrils. After resting a few minutes, we saw that the only way out was via the way he came in. There was a back current along one side, but it was also deep. When the horse got to there he again disappeared. We pulled his head up, but couldn't get him to move. With no ears, he looked like an old alligator lying there with only his eyes and nose sticking out of the water. After what seemed like an eternity, with us laughing and the Stevens kids bawling, Old Croppy lunged up and bit off a bunch of green willow leaves and never slowed down. In a couple of more lunges, he was able to get his footing a climbed out.

Picture: John (twelve years-old) and Old Sparky

In the wintertime the scene changed to ice skating. Our crowd grew to include the Robb and Smith boys. Many is the night we used to play hockey by moonlight using an old milk can for a puck. I learned to skate on old clamp-on skates. When I got my first pair of shoe skates, I was ecstatic. I could try anything without fear of a skate coming off. One time John and I, Elton Robb, Fred and Rawlin Smith challenged a whole crowd of city boys, all older than we were and we beat them soundly in a game of hockey. Sometimes John and I would skate to school on the canal (about seven miles). We had so much fun on the farm that it was hard to remember all the adversities like the bitter cold winters, hauling ice for water, walking to school when the snow drifts were too high for the bus to run or chopping holes in the ice to water the stock.

When I was about fourteen or fifteen, we had a big Wyoming blizzard and the winds were blowing about sixty mph. John and I rode the school bus and then walked the quarter of a mile to the house. John beat me home. I saw dad in his sheepskin coat with Old Stubby pulling the ice sled. When he first called to me, I ignored him. My first thought was that he was going to get ice, but he had brought me a coat and boots. He told me to get into the ice barrel which was full of quilts and warm stuff. It sure felt good.

It was a thrill to shoot my first deer and elk and I will always remember my first trip into Devil's Canyon. Henry was with me when I shot my first elk. Dad, Henry and I left the farm early one morning in November and intended to go up on the Big Horn Mountain to hunt. At the foot of the mountain, we saw fresh elk tracks in the snow heading up a canyon. We followed them. Dad stayed on one side of the canyon; Henry on the other. I followed their tracks up through the timber in the bottom. I was so eager and enthusiastic following the tracks that I got ahead of Dad and Henry and near the top, I ran into a herd of about ten or twelve elk. They began to scatter, but I was able to shoot two of them.

Henry was a great hunter. He was soon there to show me how to clean them. Dad came and was proud that I had shot them, but chewed on me for getting so far ahead. Henry and Dad started dragging the meat out to the Hang Over trail and sent me back to the farm to get John and Old Kit, our workhorse with a harness. It was a lot of work for that day, but I think I was walking on cloud nine.

When we lived in Lovell it was almost a tradition that we would go to the Yellowstone Park to fish on Memorial Day. This particular day we stopped at Steam Boat Point. Henry and I both got into a little one-man raft and started fishing. About fifty yards from shore, Henry went to make a long cast and upset the boat. The water was ice cold and we nearly froze as we clung to the raft and paddled back to shore. After building a fire and getting dry and warm, I will never forget how good the trout tasted the way Henry cooked them. Cooking over an open fire in the mountains was nothing new for Henry.

On one occasion, Dad and all five of his sons went on a fishing trip to Yellowstone. At that time we could camp anywhere we chose and catch a limit of ten fish each. The fishing was good. After keeping what we needed for camp, we buried our limit in a large snowbank to take home later. They were beautiful Yellowstone cutthroat trout weighing about one to one and a half pounds each. One evening, Dad was fixing supper with more fish than we could eat when Henry came into camp with half of a watermelon. He traded the melon for fish. We were enjoying that when John came in with the other half of the same melon he had traded for. It was really a fun outing around the campfire and superb fishing. We all learned a lot about fly fishing from Dad and Henry. On the way home, we stopped at the snow drift to pick up the fish we had stashed only to find a bear had beat us to the fish. The trip with our dad and the lessons learned were invaluable.

One particular year, John and I were left to put in the crops and do the farming while Dad and my other brothers were away shearing sheep. I was surprised and elated when Henry gave me his Model T Ford and twenty dollars for the work I had done on the farm. Henry has always been very kind and generous. We figured the old car was worth about $10.00.

One winter when we were teenagers, John and I were left alone on the farm. Dad had taken a job away and Aunt Emma spent her winters in Utah with her own children. For staying alone, we got to keep all the cream money (about $4.50 a week) and what we could get for the eggs after buying our school supplies. Henry was always there to oversee and about once a week we would enjoy a good meal up at Henry and Geneva's. During this winter of great prosperity of milk and egg money, we bought each other a pair of shoe ice skates for Christmas.

One day, we went ice skating up on the Deaver reservoir and found the ice to be about two feet thick. In the middle of the lake, there was a high spot that became an island when the water was low. This year the lake had frozen over when the water was high, and as the water lowered it left a shelf of ice four feet higher than the rest of the lake. John and I had great fun skating as fast as we could and seeing how far we could jump off this ledge. That night after supper and chores, Henry took us back to Deaver where we met the Rob and Smith boys. It was a perfect moonlit night for ice skating. After skating around and having fun, someone suggested playing follow the leader. We all took off following John. Henry was last and the only one not knowing where the drop off was. We all made the jump safely and circled around to see Henry crash and burn. He vowed to get even someday.

It was a beautiful fall morning in late November that my friend and neighbor, Heber Rob, and I decided we would like to go for a horseback ride. We saddled up our two riding horses, Old Lightfoot and Fly, and started for a place called Bear Canyon in the Pryor Mountains. On such a clear day the mountains looked much closer than they really were (about 15 miles). We enjoyed the ride as we crossed the big blue hill and into the cedars that grew profusely on the red hill. We passed the area where petroglyphs had been chiseled into the rocks anciently. We paused there for a few minutes to eat a honey sandwich and an apple and enjoy the warm sun and the smell of the scrub elders and sage brush. It was afternoon and we were only half way there, but determined to get to our destination. We rode hard for the next few hours, up through cedar breaks and little canyons of the Montana Bad Lands. It was late afternoon when we finally reached the mouth of Bear Canyon just to say we had been there. As night comes early that time of year, we looked for an easier way home. From where we sat on our horses we could see a little canyon that went through the rough Bad Lands; then opened up into comparatively flat land and easy ride from there. We chose to ride that way. We were almost through the canyon and could see the level ground on the other side. The rock walls of the canyon came quite close together, but there was a small game trail on a little rock ledge about three feet higher than the very bottom of the canyon that was full of large broken rock fragments. I would have to lead Old Lightfoot on this narrow ledge for about twenty feet where he could jump down about two feet onto level ground. That was a bad mistake. About halfway along his hind feet slipped off the trail and into the bottom. In trying to get him to back up, I only managed to tip him upside down in the narrow creek bottom. There he was upside down with a straight up and down wall of rock on one side, the little ledge on the other. All four feet were helplessly in the air with his saddle among the big rocks. He was wedged in so tight he could not move. I cut the belly band of the saddle to free him of it, then using the bridle reins and parts of Heber's saddle, we tried to devise a means by which we could pull him upright using the other horse. It didn't work. I only managed to get kicked in the head. This opened a wound in my scalp that bled profusely. This ended our endeavors to rescue the horse. We retired from the scene a short distance and built a fire as it was now getting quite dark. It was decided that it would be best if Heber rode for help and I would stay by the fire as I was sick and hurt. The mental anguish was worse than the pain. This was John's horse, and why should he be punished for my stupid blunder? I had seen other farm animals trapped on their back and they didn't live long. As Heber left to go to his horse, I knelt and prayed. I could not have been more humble and sincere. I prayed that the horse would be kept alive and that Heber could return safely with help. I also made promises to the Lord that I would obey the word of wisdom and would always uphold the standards of the church. For a few moments, I was comforted.

It was as though a warm blanket of God's love was spread over me. This feeling of relaxation and comfort was short lived when I heard Heber holler "Come on Jared; let's go home." I just knew that could only mean one thing—the horse must be dead. I gingerly made my way down to the scene. The moon was now up and what I saw was unbelievable. There was Old Lightfoot standing beside the other horse as if nothing had happened. Only the broken saddle reminded us of the dire predicament we were in only a short time before. This proved to me the fact "there is nothing impossible for the Lord." We had truly seen a miracle.

The significance of this occasion has affected my entire life, only sometimes in review, I can see times in my life where I have needed another kick in the head for some of the foolish things I have done. I pray for forgiveness. I can truly say that I have kept the vows I made at that time. I have never puffed on a cigarette or tasted liquor of any kind and have a firm testimony of the truthfulness of the gospel.

In 1982 (forty-six years later) on a trip to Wyoming, my wife Marie and I borrowed my brother Earl's pickup and went in search of the place where the horse was stuck in the rocks. We found the spot, but the canyon floor has filled in and it would be no trouble to ride a horse through. We found where Heber and I had built the fire under the pine tree. Some of the charred black coals of the fire lay among the pine needles. I have kept one of those coals as a souvenir. I knelt and prayed to thank the Lord for all the goodness he had shown me and for the opportunities that lie ahead. Marie took pictures, but I was surprised to see her crying because the spirit was so strong.

Picture: Jared in prayer at place of miracle

The first tractor on our farm was an International F-12. That was a small three-wheel tractor with steel wheels. It seemed large then. It could do the work of about a four horse team. I was delighted to run it after cranking it to get it started. I remember it had two fuel tanks, one for gasoline to get it started and after it warmed up you would switch it to the other tank with tractor fuel.

One day I was bringing it home from the upper farm. The road was on the canal bank. Having only one wheel in front it could make a very short turn, but with no power steering, it was hard and slow to make a turn. I thought I had this problem solved when I put a suicide knob on the steering wheel. Then I could spin the tractor around easily with one hand. I was getting pretty cocky with my new toy.

I had it in high gear when Grant Smith and a bunch of kids from town on their way to go swimming at our swimming hole, came up behind me. When Grant honked his horn I was a little startled, but there was enough room to pass so I gave the steering wheel a whip only to have the knob on the wheel come off in my hand. In less than a second, the tractor was upside down in the canal and I was a very wet and embarrassed young man. We had to get a wrecker from town to come and pull it out. John and I worked until late at night getting it all drained out and new oil put in it. I missed a date with Elna that night on account of the accident. Rex picked up our girls and came to see John and I cleaning up the old tractor. Henry's only remark was "Serves you right for trying to show off."

I was seventeen when I started to date. My first date was with Elna. We had planned on going to the Junior Prom in Byron but ended up going to a movie because her feet were too sore to dance. She had marched with the band at a music festival the day before. I dated a few other girls, but none of them appealed to me as Elna did. She was very smart and could ride like the wind on Old Coaly. All the other girls seemed helpless and just got in the way. I could have a lot more fun with the guys.

Old White Church House - Cowley

Community Hall

The year I was sixteen, I was a senior in high school. Elna and her friends were sophomores. All four years of seminary met together during the school year, but we continued to meet as members of the Jr. Genealogy during the summer. The next two years we planned trips to the temple in Cardston, Alberta, Canada, which was our temple district to do baptisms for the dead. It was fun raising money for meals and motels at night. We hired the school bus that would haul about eighteen of us and small handbags. One year, my sister Katie was our leader. The next year, Opal Harston was our leader and the bishop, her husband, was our chaperone. The girls sat on one side of the bus and the boys sat on the other. We would sing and joke and have a good time as we traveled. We thought it smart to call the nine girls the ten tribes. It went with the lessons we had been studying in seminary. That name, the ten tribes, identified that group for years after.

During that trip while driving Lis Harston had baked a large batch of cookies and was passing them out. When she came to Mary Alice Marchant, Mary Alice said, "I want two because I am hungry." The boys picked that up and gave her the nickname of "Old Hungry". She was probably the prettiest girl, but very thin. In fact, she was so skinny she would have to walk in the bright sunlight twice to even cast a shadow. She would always walk to school and you would often hear one of the boys holler "Here comes Old Hungry". This would infuriate her and she tried to catch them. The boys liked to be chased by the prettiest girl in town. I never learned until many years later that she would go home at night and cry because her friends thought she was someone to laugh at. I am ashamed that I was one of those boys.

The 10 tribes

Top row: Virjene Stevens and Flora Baird; third row: Elna Lewis, Marie Mathews and May Alice Marchant; second row: Verda Stevens, Virginia Welch and Nellie Welch (not related to Virginia); front row: Geneva Stevens (related to Virjene)

Mary Alice Marchant

We stayed the first night in Great Falls, Montana, where we had cabins. The next day the hilarity and jokes continued until we got to McGrath and my Aunt Vie and Uncle Jack Bridge's home, which was thirty miles from Cardston. They set up two big tents on a large lot. The girls were on one side of the house and the boys were on the other. The bishop and his wife had a nice bedroom in the house.

The next day we put on our Sunday clothes and prepared to go to the temple. President Woods was the temple president. He gave us an address. All the nonsense we had the day before was gone. The girls looked like little angels in their nice clothes; even more so as they changed into white to do the baptisms.

It was during President Woods talk that we really felt the spirit of the Holy Ghost. He asked us what we had been learning. He called on Ray Harston to tell what he had been learning. My heart sank. To my amazement Ray answered every question correctly, and I am sure he couldn't have done it without the help of the Holy Ghost. He said afterward, he just happened to remember everything that the President asked. That was a real miracle.

Back home, we were called to the different wards in our towns of Lovell, Cowley, and Byron to give a report of our temple trip. Mary Alice Marchant, Betty Jo Crosby, and Geena Welling always accompanied us to sing in a trio. They also sang at a lot of the assemblies in the different schools. The temple made a huge impact on our lives.

One of the best assignments I had in the church was being an ordinance worker in the temple for eleven and a half years in my later years. One of the most spiritual occasion was when I was called to officiate one of the sessions. In this assignment, we were to go to the ordinance room thirty minutes before the actual session began and prepare to conduct the session in a word perfect manner. It was during this time of preparation that I felt the closest to my departed wives.

It was during the Great Depression that Henry was called to serve a mission in the southern states. It was a very difficult time for Dad to support a large family and very little money. We were lucky to have Katie teaching school and contribute a lot towards Henry's support. His mission was successful and we all benefited from it.

High school Graduation

In 1938, I was a seventeen-year old senior in high school. I had the awesome responsibility of putting in the crops and taking care of the farm while all my brothers and dad were away sheering sheep in the spring time. My brother-in-law, Kurt Karlinsey, came to help me part of the time as he worked at another job. Most of the planning and work layout was done by Dad. I followed his directions.

We had a new tractor on the farm and I spent most of my time on it, but most of the farm implements were horse drawn, like the harrow and land leveler, cultivator, and hay rake, etc. We were in bad need of another workhorse. Our neighbor Elmer Eyre said he had a three-year old that he had broken to lead, but had never put a harness or saddle on him. He said we could use him if we brought him down from the mountain pasture and broke him to work. We agreed, and I was getting ready for a trip of a lifetime.

At daylight one Monday morning, I saddled Old Lightfoot and with a long rope and a big lunch in a seamless sack Aunt Emma just made for me, I started on a long ride (about thirty-miles) for the pasture owned by Will Harston and Harry T. I left the farmlands, crossed the government canal, passed by the road to Dry Lake and started across the Wyoming Bad Lands. I met the main road from the Pryor Mountains, a road my grandfather had laid out many years before for the purpose of getting timber for the first log cabins in Cowley. About five miles further, I came to Gzo Creek and knew I was somewhere near the Montana border. It had started to rain a little, but I had the determination to keep going.

I crossed the red hills covered with cedar and scrub pine, a place where most of the Cowley folks came to gather firewood. A little further lay the white hills, a place where a lot of aquatic fossils are found. Elmer Eyre had found a few skeletal remains of dinosaurs. I picked up a few squid parts that I still have in my rock collection. At Demi John, named for a moonshine liquor jug found there, was a drift fence with a large gate the ranchers had installed. It was wild mustang habitat on both sides of the fence. I didn't see any horses, but I did see several mule deer. A little further up the road, I could look back across the valley and see the contrasting colors of the Red and White Hills and the green of the Crooked Creek Ranch and surrounding junipers. It was a magnificent sight in the now bright sunlight of the midday. It was a long hard ride mostly uphill as I entered the forest land and into the Crooked Creek Canyon that separates Pryor from East Pryor Mountain.

It was getting cloudy again as I rode past the Wyoming Campground (Old Mill Holler) and by the time I reached Tebb Holler and the old abandoned sawmill it was foggy and raining hard. As I crossed the divide and started down the other side, I left the fog and in a couple of miles the rain had stopped and I rode on to the ranch very wet and cold. My legs were chafed like fire from the wet saddle. The old barn was filled with dry Timothy hay. I pulled the saddle from Lightfoot and gave him a little bag of oats I had carried and some of the dry hay. Then I climbed into a pile of hay and the next thing I knew the sun was shining in the early morning. I was warm and even my lunch was edible.

In a herd of about thirty horses, I found the one that had been described to me. Old Darky was very dark brown and nearly black. After a few minutes, I cut him out from the herd and lassoed him and got him in tow. From there it was a long and tiring ride back home to where Aunt Emma said she was concerned and had been praying for my safety.

Picture: Jared (words on back of picture were "I'm wondering now how long it will be before Leo and I stand together by that same house in Wyoming again.")

It seemed like my world was starting to fall apart when Dad began talking about selling the farm. We had been raising sugar beets and growing hay and grain for feed. Our farm had really taken a turn for the better when we started feeding lambs in the fall and selling them in the spring. By now, the farm was mostly mechanized and even profitable. All my brothers had taken outside jobs and had left Dad and me to do it all. Dad was having serious health problems with ulcers and a bad heart. We all felt that if he stayed on the farm, it would probably kill him. With his problem firmly in mind, I had to make a very important decision. I had thought of joining the Navy but was quite confused. I decided to ask the Lord, so I prayed for an hour or more and suddenly it all came clear to me that Dad had a great work to do in the temple and that I could better serve circumstances if I joined the United States Navy.

The night passed slowly as I lie awake many hours dreaming over my many memories and all the things my father had taught me. I could see the farm as though it was laid out on a map and every square inch of it reminded me of something that will never be forgotten. I could see my brothers coming in from work, and Dad and Aunt Emma there to greet them and learn of the day's progress. I could see Old Tip and Lightfoot and could remember the many times John and I had been together herding cows, ice skating, hunting and fishing. We had even planned on owning the farm together as partners, but with good times on the coast and the need for more money to support his oncoming family, John had engaged in other work. I did not feel sorry for anything I had done in my life as a farm boy, so with complete satisfaction, I said a prayer of goodbye to everything and closed my eyes to the many fond memories.

The following morning, Dad called me over to talk with him as he had done many times, but this time, I knew it was for a special reason. He said, "Son, you have got to make good, remember who you are, and what you are. If you don't, I will never be able to face your mother after sending you away from me; and you will never be able to face her either." I had occasion to be reminded of this several times during the next few years.

A few hours later, Brother Eyre, who was in the stake presidency at that time, came up from the field and he and Dad laid their hands on my head and conferred the Melchizedek Priesthood on me and ordained me an Elder in the Church of Jesus Christ of Latter Day Saints. I was so thrilled that I cried because he gave me a wonderful blessing and I knew it was all truth if only I could live my part.

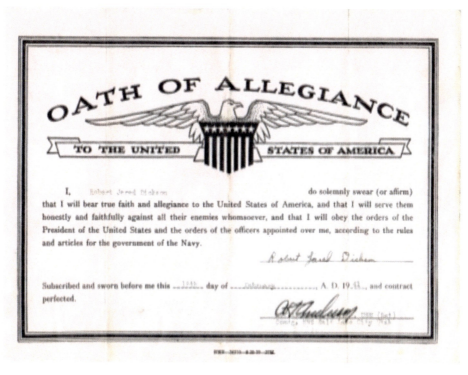

Enlistment Paper

# THE WAR

It was a cold day in Wyoming when my two close friends and I decided to go to the Navy recruiting office in Billings, Montana and investigate the possibility of enlisting. We filled out the forms and had a minor physical exam. We all qualified except Leo who was apprehensive and did not join when Heber and I did. Leo joined the day after Pearl Harbor was bombed.

Jared and Heber Robb

Jared and Leo Baird

Leo Baird

Heber and I joined several of the boys from Cowley, Lovell, and Byron, Wyoming, and took the train to Salt Lake City where we were sworn in to the USS Navy on February 19, 1941. After spending the night in the Hotel Utah, we boarded the train for San Diego. The next day and night, we traveled and were surprised to find warm skies, grass green, and tall palm trees.

We joined forty-five other boys who came from all parts of the United States to form a company led by two CPOS. We had no liberty for the first thirty days. We got haircuts, issued clothing, and shots, and were examined thoroughly for any kind of disease. We had to wash our own clothing and learn how to store it in a sea bag, which consisted of a hammock, bedding and clothes that all were arranged precisely the same. It was displayed on our bunks for inspection day, but stored in a foot locker the rest of the time. The next few weeks we marched, paraded, learned the manual of arms, discipline, and just what the Navy was in general. The part that impressed me the most was three good meals and regular hours for work and sleep. I gained twenty pounds in the next four weeks and fifty pounds in four months. We were paid $21 per month and $3 was taken out for insurance.

At the end of training, we were given an aptitude exam to see who would qualify for a trade school. About half of the company flunked out completely, but Heber and I qualified and chose to take a class in metalwork. This class lasted for four months and included welding, soldering, and logging, along with drafting, sheet metal layout and blueprint reading. I graduated with a 3.91 GPA and the training proved invaluable in my later career. During this time, of schooling, I would get liberty every night and on weekends. That gave me time to go to church and every Saturday night a class was held for the service men and women and all the local ward and stake leaders. I got acquainted with a nice girl who was only sixteen. She was fun to visit with or walk in the park. Her mother invited me to dinner a couple of times. It was fun, but no one could compare with Elna.

On September 3rd, 1941, I got a fifteen-day leave and immediately headed for Wyoming. I stopped at Laramie to see Elna and Jay and some of the other guys. I went straight to where Jay and Glenn were staying and was really glad to see them. I got all spruced up and went to Mutual where I expected to meet Elna. I met Ray and Marlow Harston and some of the girls from home. I was talking to Jay when Elna walked in. I was so glad to see her I could have burst, and you could have knocked her over with a feather. She said that in four months I had changed from a boy into a man. I had grown two inches and gained fifty pounds. After hello and a long warm handshake, we talked of this and that and nothing until M.I.A. started. We stayed for opening exercises and then skipped classes and went uptown for our special treat that we had enjoyed many times before (a frosty malt). We had a good visit, and I learned that she had never forgiven me for the time I broke a date with her because of the time I had to work late to get the tractor out of the canal and cleaned up. I hated it like fury when I had to kiss her goodbye again for who knows how long.

Helen Baird (married John Dickson), Jared and Elna Lewis Dickson and Earl Dickson (Jared's brother)

The next day I reached home in Cowley. It was a cold blustery day so I went to take refuge in the post office while waiting for Katie. I had to remove a few tumbleweeds to get in the door. I was sure glad to see Katie. Leo was running the filling station so I saw him and then went to find John. He was working at the canning factory, driving trucks. I stopped his truck along the road and we both jumped out and started shaking hands too emotional to say anything for a minute or two.

The next day, I put on my old clothes and went to Robbs to say hello to everyone. After that, I went over to the old farm to look around. It sure made me homesick to see the place so neglected. The house was not being lived in and weeds were shoulder high in the yard. As I looked at the old farm, a million memories sprang to mind. Newell told me how John had broken down once when he came back from Tacoma and saw the farm in other hands. My heart was heavy and I was about to do the same thing.

The next few days, we went hunting up on the North Fork. John and I, Elton, Leo and George were there and Henry came up the following day. We stayed in a cabin and really had fun. Most of us got our own meat.

On the way back to the U.S.N., I stayed at Dad's place in Salt Lake City. I found them both well and happy. Dad was engrossed temple work and Aunt Emma was near her family. They both came down to the bus station to see me off.

After the leave, I went back to San Diego and checked into a receiving ship waiting for further orders. While there, I was put on a mine sweeper. As first mate, we would patrol the harbor at daylight towing a mine catching device. It was all routine. We never detected or caught any mines. By 8:00 am, we would be through and have the rest of the day and night off. I had plenty of liberty. They had all kinds of recreational facilities, and I was able to go to church. For several weeks, I went to work in a nearby shipyard in my spare time to earn $2.00 an hour as a welder. I would have been happy to stay there and earn the big bucks, but it was quite exciting to see my name on a draft for overseas. It was with mixed emotions when we mustered with a draft to ship out on the U.S.S. Tippycanoe.

When I went aboard the ship, I had advanced in rating from seaman to first class eireman with a raise in pay to $36 per month. I was assigned to work in the metal shop as a welder and blacksmith and engineer of a motor daindy when in port. I soon took the tests and advanced to the rate of metalsmith petty officer and a raise in pay to $72 per month.

We shoved off for Pearl Harbor. This trip was the longest, roughest and most unappreciated trip of my whole career. It was my first time at sea and the third day out we hit a storm that sent waves over the superstructure decks. One hundred passengers were in the forward hold and it was too rough to even open the hatch for ventilation. Everyone was sick and heaving their toes. The place smelled like a pigpen as the vomit and sea water accumulated to about four inches deep on the steel deck that sent everything and everybody sliding from one bulkhead to the other in heavy seas. It lasted three days before it calmed down. It took the remainder of the nine-day trip to clean up the mess and get things aired out. It was calm and beautiful as we pulled into Pearl Harbor on November 26, 1941.

I was really impressed by the magnitude of the U.S. fleet. The battleships were all tied up to the docks on the east side of Ford Island. As we pulled in they were retrieving colors and all hands were in white uniforms. Two days later I was transferred to the U.S.S. Curtiss, a seaplane tender, for permanent duty. I was assigned as engineer of a motor launch and worked out of the metal shops as welder mostly while at sea. The Curtiss was a fairly large ship displacing 35,000 tons of water and had a ship crew of 900 men. It was new and clean and quite a contrast to the old oil tanker, Tippycanoe.

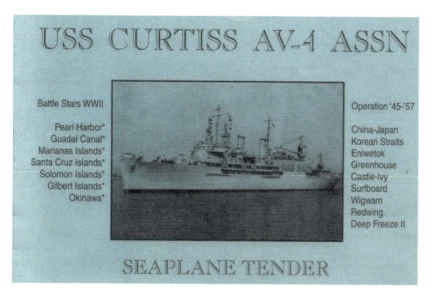

# USS CURTISS AV-4 ASSN

**Battle Stars WWII**

Pearl Harbor*
Guadal Canal*
Marianas Islands*
Santa Cruz Islands*
Solomon Islands*
Gilbert Islands*
Okinawa*

**Operation '45-'57**

China-Japan
Korean Straits
Eniwetok
Greenhouse
Castle-Ivy
Surfboard
Wigwam
Redwing
Deep Freeze II

## SEAPLANE TENDER

USS Curtiss

The battleship, USS Nevada took our berth on battleship row so the USS Curtiss moved to the west side of Ford Island and moored to a buoy. We would have been an easy target for the Japanese torpedo planes had we stayed where we were. We sailed from Pearl Harbor over to the Big Island at Hilo and were really impressed by the beauty of the islands. We had liberty there and a few of us climbed the side of a still active volcano, Mauna Kea. We returned to Pearl Harbor the night of December 6 and moored the ship to a buoy about 200 yards out on the west side of Ford Island.

December 7, 1941, was a bright sunny Sabbath morning. We had reveille as usual, but half of the crew still lay in the bunks. Being Sunday, it was a scheduled holiday routine on the ship. I had the day's duty in the boats and had made one trip to shore. I tied the boat up to the boat boom and came aboard for breakfast. I had just sat down to eat when I heard a few loud explosions. "What the heck is that?" I wondered and saw a few guys around the portholes looking and hollering to each other. I dashed over just in time to see several Japanese planes swoop across the landing strip on Ford Island and drop their bombs on the hangers.

General Quarters was sounded and we all dashed to our battle stations to set up a defense. My battle station was amid ship repair in the after mess hall. I wore a headgear with two-way communications to keep the crew advised of pertinent information. It was scary to be below decks and feel the rocking of the ship as she fired her guns and to hear the explosions of the nearby bomb blasts. Our whip was hit and it put out the lights and filled our compartment with smoke. They passed the word on the P.A. for all boat crews to man their boats and cast off and be prepared to pick up survivors. I went to the boat deck looking for my crew and while there I saw a plane shot down and crash 200 yards away on the beach. I also saw the finish of a two-man submarine fifty yards off our starboard quarter. Our crew on a 50 caliber machine gun had shot its periscope off and as it tried to surface, they hit it directly in the conning tower with a five-inch shell. A destroyer underway rammed it a glancing blow and as it slid by the destroyer dropped a depth charge on it. I saw the broken sub come completely out of the water and sink in a mass of rubble.

My boat crew was either on gun crew or otherwise detained so I took the boat alone. In the bay, I was discouraged by bombs, shrapnel and machine gun fire. I misjudged when I thought I could cross the bay in front of two destroyers making their way out of the channel. I was ahead of one, but would have collided with the second. I turned abruptly as the ships sped by on either side. I was directly between them when Japanese planes made a run at them, firing machine guns and dropping bombs. I ducked into the bow of the boat and heard the bullets slap into the water all around me. It was over in seconds, and I was not surprised to see holes in my boat. But I was surprised to find myself in one piece, just scared and wet.

The U.S.S Utah was torpedoed and rolled over. I saw men and timbers falling off her in complete devastation. I made my way across the bay, dodging the Utah's debris. I rescued a man clinging to the timbers who was almost frozen in shock. On the beach, there was a little cement house that we climbed into and seemed to be safe from the bombs that hit so closely they literally lifted us off the floor. The windows were all shattered by shrapnel. There would be a silence of several minutes and then a few seconds of attack as the planes came to our side of the island again, dropping their bombs and strafing personnel.

During the lull, we would venture out and try to see what was happening elsewhere. One time, I saw an explosion a quarter of a mile away that nearly knocked me down. I thought it must have been an ammunition dump, but later we found out that the Shaw was hit in the forward magazine. I saw great fires and heard great explosions as torpedo planes dropped their loads on the battleship row.

Another group of planes came our way, and we jumped back into our little house. After a few seconds of deafening booms, one of the fellows hollered "The Curtiss is hit!"

I looked out to see a Japanese plane with one wing shot off crash into the ship and spread fire from the boat deck to the forecastle. Almost simultaneously a bomb exploded in the hanger deck and I saw great billows of smoke pouring out over the main deck aft. By this time, I wasn't scared, but very angry because there was nothing I could do about it at all.

After an unusually long lull, we thought the raid was over and had gone outside to look the situation over when *Boom!* a bomb had hit just barely on the other side of a small hill from us. We looked up to see the Japanese planes at about 5,000 feet.

By now, all the ships that were able and all the shore batteries had put up anti-aircraft fire forcing the Japanese to climb for safety. They had done their damage anyway. A few more explosions and the raid was over.

We felt a little safer this time as we walked out and watched for our recall signal. The Curtiss was listing heavily to the starboard, and we thought it was about to capsize. Four of us got in a motor launch and returned to the ship. They were still at general quarters and fighting fires so we left again and went out around the bay to take the dead and body parts to hospital landing and the badly wounded to the hospital ship, Solace. After a little while, other boats came to help us with this grizzly task.

What we saw was total chaos and destruction. We went past the Utah as she lay upside down exposing her keel and both screws. The Nevada was on the beach with smoke spilling out of the forward hold. The Arizona looked as if her back was broken as she lay nearly submerged enveloped in flames and heavy black smoke. The entire battleship row was a pile of junk. The West Virginia was higher out of the water, but it also was on the bottom. It was burning fiercely as were all the others and also the surrounding docks and oil that was on the water. The Tennessee, Pennsylvania, and Maryland were listing and afire. They were protected from torpedoes by the other ships but were badly damaged by bombs and fire. The Oklahoma was completely upside down. To say the least, the damage was extensive.

Cruising around the bay looking for survivors and bodies, we plowed through fuel oil three and four inches thick and smoke so thick we often had to move out for fresh air for a few minutes and then return to pick up the mutilated bodies.

Eventually, we returned to our own ship and found a big job for us there. I found out that 2 of my friends and several others I had worked with in midship repairs had been killed in the original bomb hit. Altogether, twenty-eight were killed on our ship. I went aboard and helped carry casualties down to the boat. Seven fellows were caught in a flash fire in #4 handling room and were so badly burned their bodies could not be identified. They had to be shoveled into sacks. One fellow,

"Warich," had half of his foot missing and had so much morphine he didn't feel the pain. He saw me staring at his foot and said, "Don't worry about that, that foot had spic itch anyway." We learned later that he died from shock and loss of blood.

That night we took the boats and spent the night on the beach. We had rifles and were prepared to use them. All that night every gun emplacement on the island would test their guns. Every few minutes a rat-a-tat-tat of a machine gun or a pom-pom of a 40 mm would break the dreaded silence and send tracers into the black night.

Death and destruction had come to our Navy. I thought that three or four thousand men had surely died. We also heard the damages and casualties were high at Hickam Field and also at the Schofield marine barracks where the men were caught in the mess hall. Every morning at daylight was spent at general quarters and every night was blacked out completely.

The Japanese never came back.

Navy, Company 41 A

 

    The USS Curtiss was badly damaged and we spent six weeks in the Navy yard getting repaired. We came back to San Diego for supplies and a load of aviation fuel for the planes, then the trip back to Pearl Harbor where we picked up admiral staff and more supplies in preparation for deployment to the South Seas. We were escorted by the USS Detroit as we followed a zig zag course. The first stop was at Christmas Island. We sailed between there and Pago Pago, Samoa. We were called to our battle stations and were notified that the cruiser Detroit had surprised a Japanese submarine on the surface and had sunk it.

As we pulled into the harbor at Pago Pago, I think all the youth of that island swam out to greet us. They would dive for coins that we tossed for them. It was quite impressive.

We crossed the equator and the International Date Line the same day. While crossing the equator the ship stopped, and an invitation was given to all us pollywogs to go swimming. We continued on to Espiritu Santo in the New Hebrides Islands where we stationed as a base of operation for our planes (the PBY). The admirals also planned their operations for the battle of the Coral Seas and Guadalcanal. Our planes would take off early in the morning and return in the afternoon and evening. The PBY was a slow cumbersome plane used mostly for reconnaissance and rescue. They could take off and land at sea, but they were also used as fighters and torpedo planes in the early part of the war. Their casualties were great. I personally saw one plane with holes in its hull come up to the ship and sank before they could hook on to it with the crane to lift it out of the water.

The life aboard ship was quite routine. We worked at our special on duty watch which was in the vaporize area where we made potable water from seawater. If not on watch, there was a free time after chow time until lights went out around 9:30 p.m. This gave us time to go to the library and write letters, etc. A lot of the guys would gather in groups on the main deck aft to smoke and play cards and tell dirty jokes. A lot would talk about drinking and bragging about how many notches they had with girls in every port. I found this disgusting. One loud mouthed character came to the group I was with and yelled at the top of his voice, letting everyone on deck know that I was a Mormon and too chicken to even smoke a cigarette. This made me mad. I got to my feet and shoved him against the guard rail and held him there. I said to him, *one cigarette would probably do me no harm so I will make you a deal. I will smoke one today and one every day for six weeks if you will go six weeks without smoking. We will see who is the chicken.* When a couple of my buddies came to my side, I let him go. He went away muttering, "These *** Mormons." That incident made me a lot of new friends, and he avoided me from then on.

Sunday Group: Jared Dickson, Horace Rapley, Niles Misery, Del Stevens

Del Stevens, 2 teachers, Jared Dickson

Latter-Day Saint group in Hawaii

Jared at Hawaii Stake Center

While in the New Hebrides, the workday was mostly routine working in the metal shop and other welding projects around the ship, but at least once a week I got to go with the diving crew on practices. I would often go ashore looking for fruit and swim in a nearby river.

Horace Rapley, Del Stevens and Jared

Jared and Eddy Dion at Hawaiian Temple

I was also on the ship's diving crew. We practiced diving every week. This was before the scuba gear was invented, and we only had the head gear attached to hoses that supplied the air from a boat with an air compressor that was cranked by hand. The deepest I ever ventured was thirty feet. The only official dive we made while I was there was on the USS Tucker that had hit a mine and sunk in shallow water. The mast was still visible and the bridge and chart house was twelve to twenty-one feet under water. We would dive wearing only goggles and flippers and return things from the drawers and cabinets. I got so I could stay under water for two minutes. For the most part of my diving career, we just practiced. One time I found a huge clam that weighed about fifty pounds. I brought it aboard ship and the officers had a meal of it. I was invited to their mess. Our chief engineer kept the shell and displayed it at his home in Seattle when he retired.

One day when I had boat duty, the Chaplin and a few others chose to go to a nearby island and visit a plantation. One sailor he chose could speak French fluently. The people who lived there spoke French. As we approached, the Chaplain told us not to be surprised at what we saw. The headquarters of the plantation was a sanctuary of some kind of religion. As we pulled into the lagoon a bunch of native teenagers came to the dock to help us land the boat. We were surprised to see they all wore the same outfits, probably uniforms to signify their religion. They were all topless, even the well-developed girls. After communicating with them, the French-speaking sailor and the Chaplain left us to go into the office building. The kids showed us how to wade out in the lagoon and look for pretty seashells. I still have some of them. As we were about to leave they brought us out a drink made from oranges, grapefruit, mangos, and papaya. It was delicious. It was fun, and I thought it would be nice to go back there some day after the war.

After about two years in the bay at Espiritu Santo, I remember seeing our planes getting fueled and prepared for leaving at daylight and counting them as they returned in the afternoon. I was there when the USS Coolidge struck a mine in the channel and ran aground. When I saw it, only the bow was in sight, but as it took on water in less than one hour it slid into the deep water and sank.

I was there when Leo Baird's ship, the USS Hayes, came into the harbor, and we both got leave for a few hours. We went ashore and visited. His ship had just returned from the Battle of Guadalcanal and Tulagi. He was on deck manning a twenty-millimeter gun when an enemy dive bomber made a run at his ship. He saw one bomb fall fifty short and the second bomb miss the other side of the ship. It was close enough that the spray of the explosion got him wet. That plane was shot down, but he wasn't sure he had hit it.

While there in the New Hebrides, we saw the Seabees come in and clear enough jungle to build an airfield and barrack large enough to handle the B17 and B24 bombers. It seemed the use of our old PBY planes had about outlived their usefulness.

During this time, I contacted an unidentified disease they called "jungle itch". I got an infection in my ears and ankles, and my belt line would swell and blister and itch like crazy; something like Shingles. They took me off the duty list and kept me in the sick bay for a couple of days.

After a long time in one place, the USS Curtiss finally pulled anchor and started on a long journey toward the United States of America. We made brief stops at New Caledonia, the Fiji Islands and then on to Tonga. It was near the Tongan Islands that we encountered a typhoon. The ship pulled between two small islands and dropped both anchors to ride out the storm. They measured the wind at 130 – 145 mph. We had to keep both engines turning at 1/3 forward to keep from blowing aground. Other smaller ships didn't do as well and swamped or washed ashore. Before we reached the Tongan Islands a supply ship met us alongside and transferred supplies. It had been a long time since we had real eggs and milk and fresh fruit and vegetables. The meat was mostly mutton (sheep).

In Tonga, we had a few hours of liberty just to go ashore to visit the fish market and other attractions on display. One interesting thing we saw was a native boy about eight or ten-years-old riding on a large sea turtle. They said the turtle was over one hundred years old.

From Tonga, our next stop was an island called Funafuti. As we approached we were called to our battle stations. There had been an enemy air strike on the island only thirty minutes before we got there.

From Tonga we started on our long journey home. We sailed over towards Chile and then we sailed up the coast towards San Francisco. From there we pulled into Alameda. Then I was transferred to the naval hospital in Oakland. I was there for about a week and got a transfer to the naval hospital in Seattle where I underwent different tests. They diagnosed it as angioneurotic edema (whatever that is). It apparently had something to do with the hot, continuous weather. I was in the hospital for about a month. My transfer was to Dutch Harbor. I went aboard a merchant ship as a passenger. The ship supplied all the fish canneries along the way. We went through the Inland Passage and the entire trip took seven days. While I was in the process of being transferred the Navy shut down the marine base at Dutch Harbor and I was left in limbo. Because of my rank, I was transferred to a repair ship.

I spent time at Adak, Alaska, and was assigned to a repair ship. The rumors were that we were to follow the fleet into the invasion of Japan. It was on this ship that I was still in the harbor when we got word that bombs had been dropped on Japan and they had surrendered. This started a wholesale celebration. All the gun emplacements and ships in the habor fired their guns and flare guns. The guns fired into the sea.

The flares went into the hillside and started a fire in the tall, dead grass. We had to go ashore and fight fires until almost midnight.

Within a few days we headed back to the United States. At this time I put in a request for being discharged early. When I got back to Bremerton I was assigned to go aboard a destroyer, the USS Henderson and my duties were Master of Arms and my watch was on the throttle when at sea and patrolling the living quarters when in port. I was responsible for getting all the sailors up at reveille in the morning. The destroyer was brand new and had a top speed of about 30. In the rough waters it would dive into the big waves and the decks were awash with sea coming overboard. It seems like we would dive under one big wave and ride over the top of the next one. It was a rough ride. The Henderson was still undergoing tests. We went to sea at day and returned at night. The last day I went to sea, the ship was being deployed to the South Seas. We still had some of the engineers and repairmen aboard. We had to bring them back into port. That night in the mail call were my orders for discharge, but the mail wasn't opened until the next morning. When we were underway my orders for discharge were in the mail. The ship pulled into Bangor Island and I was put ashore and was to report back to Bremerton. I took the letter and hitchhiked back to Bremerton where I was assigned again to a receiving ship and spent a couple of weeks with no duty and plenty of liberty; waiting for the draft that would send me to a discharge station. The first draft I was listed at was New York. I deliberately missed that. I got new orders to go to Shoemaker, CA where I was discharged.

Elna was still in the Waves and still on duty in San Francisco as a supply officer. She knew where I was all during the war. I got to visit with her until the day I was discharged.

The following is a poem I wrote called "Away Out in the Ocean".

Across the foaming brine
We had the goodly notion
To escape the worldly clime.

We packed our bags so neatly
And in the dark of night
We forsook our cares completely
As we took the early flight.

Across the ocean wide and blue
We flew with lightning speed
To where people good and true
See greatly to our need.

The water and air are clean and pure.
To this we can attest.
Where we can escape our worldly cares
And gain our needed rest.

We snorkeled where the turtles are

And followed all the rules.
Our hearts are full as we crossed the bar
And saw fishes in their schools.

The trade winds blow from across the isle
And from the sleepy sea.
It brings peace of mind and all the while
A sense of peace to me.

Many years before on this peaceful shore
I saw the serenity shattered,
Where enemy planes came swooping in
And ships and men were battered.

The enemy then is now our friend
As all enmity has ended.
All is well on the peaceful shore
With the evil Warlords apprehended.

Now down in the deep our heroes sleep
As if in a cool rose arbor.
Their legacy now for us to keep
Is to REMEMBER PEARL HARBOR.

Memories shall linger on

In the hearts of us now living.
Let us do our part with a cheerful heart
And consider a true forgiving.

Let us live in a land our fathers built
Through righteous toil and pain.
Let us live in a way that is free from guilt
Where the love of Christ could reign.

# ELNA

In 1945, I was discharged from the Navy and started finding my way to choose an occupation and get acclimated to civilian life.

I went immediately to John and Helen's home where they lived in Tacoma. They had two little boys, Lynn and Jack. Little Doris was born about a month later. John was working in the shipyards, but there seemed to be nothing really attractive for me to do.

Earl and Henry had left the shipyards and had worked for Uncle Owen a few years at the White River Lumber Company near Enumclaw, Washington. They had just purchased a welding shop in Lovell, Wyoming, and that sort of thing interested me. I invested what money I had saved while in the navy and went into partnership with them. I never consulted Elna about this venture and soon learned that she did not approve. Elna and one of my best friends convinced me that I should go to school at the University of Wyoming.

I really enjoyed my stay down at Laramie and the friends I had down there. They were Jay and Phyllis Partridge, Wayne Despain, Lloyd Partridge, Wayne Rollins and a host of other students. The L.D.S. Institute was always a place of refuge. All my best friends were there and we enjoyed parties, dances, ping pong, etc. The classes I took were interesting. I especially liked botany and at one time considered majoring in forestry.

For some reason, I also had the feeling that something was not complete. Some days I would find myself daydreaming and memories of the sea, the war and at times I could feel the roll of the ship and hear the whine of the ship's engines. My life seemed pretty mixed up and I felt that everything would be alright if only Elna and I could be together. The next few months that she had yet to serve in the WAVES seemed like an eternity. I had a few dates with other girls, but I knew this great feeling of discontent would never end until we could be together.

I lost interest in school and at semester break, I went back to the welding shop and pitched in trying to make a success out of that business. It seemed a never ending process trying to clean up Old Sam Egbert's accumulation of acids, mining gear and just plain junk by the truckload. I enjoyed the welding and it felt good to work with my brothers and be a part of the family again.

Elna came home for a very special time of our lives, planning our future, dates, dinners, swimming, fishing and everything fun we could think of and afford. Could it really be true that we would always be together?

Jared and Elna in uniform

In April 1946, we borrowed twenty-five dollars from Earl and Henry's 1937 Ford car and prepared for a trip to the temple to be married for time and all eternity. We drove to Dad's home in Salt Lake City and two days later, April 29, 1946, we were married in the Salt Lake temple and sealed forever. Dad and Aunt Emma were our witnesses. It was a beautiful ceremony performed by Elder Knight.

Jared and Elna on wedding day

A short honeymoon followed by way of West Yellowstone and Bozeman, Montana. We went through an endownment session in the Idaho Falls temple. Elna appeared to me as a beautiful angel.

I returned to work at the shop and Elna started immediately to build a happy family: canning, sewing, etc. We enjoyed the work and living with Elna's dad, Elroy, and it was good for him. He had been quite lonely after having lost his wife a couple of years before. Veloy, Elna's sister, was away teaching, so her brother, Mark, was the only other one of his family left at home. We spent the summer in Cowley and worked at the shop in Lovell.

It seemed my feet would never stop itching, and I had been so used to doing as I pleased that I grasped another opportunity. I heard that John had gone to work for Uncle Owen and he wanted me to come and help. Actually, there was not enough work in the welding shop to support three families, so it wasn't hard to talk Elna into the move back to Washington. Ray and Catherine Harston were moving out there too, and it seemed like a fun thing to do.

We stayed at John and Helen's for a few days and then we had our very first experience of living alone. We rented a little one room cabin at Pete's Pool near Enumclaw and lived there for about a month. Elna had her first experience with wood cook stoves. One day when I was late getting up and left for work without starting a fire, Elna attempted to build her own fire. At ten o'clock, I had to come for parts downtown and stopped at the cabin. Elna was gone. There was one large block of wood. She had really tried to build a fire but ended up having to walk to town to Helen's because it was too cold at the cabin.

We bought our first home on Merrit Street in Enumclaw. It was a beautiful home and we shared many happy remembrances there including our first Christmas, and the birth of our first child. Kathleen was born March 14, 1947. We borrowed John and Helen's car and drove to the hospital in Auburn. It was very foggy, and we were quite concerned about getting there safely and in time. We made it.

The two full-time missionaries were Elder Hanson and Elder Hegarhaurst. They joined with us playing ball and other activities and did quite well in proselyting.

We stayed in Enumclaw only a short time. My dad put pressure on me to come back and help my brothers. It broke Elna's heart when we sold our lovely home and headed back to Wyoming.

We bought our first car, a 1941 Ford, loaded it and a trailer and started for Wyoming. Around Helena, Montana we had three flat tires and had to spend all our money. The day we arrived in Cowley, it seemed like the most desolated place I had ever seen. There were no leaves, no grass, and no green of any kind. We already had second thoughts about it being the right thing to do.

Earl and Henry were out working in a field with a model of the Smith Dickson Land Leveler and Dad was with them. Dad saw me coming from across the field and met me half way to greet me and tell me it was good to have me home where I belonged.

For the next year, it was a busy time building and developing the levelers and working hard in the shop to make a living doing it. Earl, Henry and I were partners in the blacksmith shop. We called ourselves Dickson Bros. Welding. We also did a lot of radiator work. The bulk of Henry's work was with the radiators, but we all shared in the welding jobs. It was at that time we developed the Smith Dickson land leveler. The potential looked phenomenal. Fred Smith came up with the original idea, but Earl and Henry and I did all the developing and experimental work. In the business, we became involved with Fred and Rawlin Smith. Herman Krugar was hired as distributor and the sale of the first fifty machines was phenomenal. With success, bad feelings started to arise in the inequitable aspects of the contracts. The bad feelings were mostly agitated by the greed of the Smith brothers for a bigger share of the profits. This coupled with poor judgment on our part and finally the lack of enthusiasm caused us to drop out of the big business venture and continue with the welding and radiator work.

Earl took most of the credit for the invention and development of the automatic hydraulic valve that was the key to the levelers success. A number of reasons caused the breakup of this association. As busy as we were we still had time for hunting and fishing.

We lived with E. E. Lewis until fall, when bought a small house from Viv Hansen. That winter was very cold, and the gas heater was much too small for the area we had to heat so we had to light the oven in the cook stove and leave the door open for heat. This caused so much water condensation in the house that the doors swelled up and would not completely close. This let in more cold, and we turned the oven up higher. It was a vicious cycle. During the worst part of this cold spell, Kathleen, nine months old, became very ill, so much so that we called Dr. Tom Croft. She looked so sick and helpless that it scared Elna and me. We feared for her life. The doctor gave her a shot, and after he had gone, I gave her a blessing and the spirit of the Lord came over us so strong that our minds were immediately free of anxiety. Kathy's color returned and she recovered quickly. Our next investment was an adequate heater.

At this time, a young, energetic building contractor by the name of Louis B. Welch knocked on my door and offered me a job running his little dragline. For the next four years, I worked for the nicest guy in the world. I dug canals, drain ditches, sewers, etc., and helped in the erection of steel beams in the buildings. My best friend, Leo Baird, was always there running the little cat tractor, and we worked together in the houses. Other friends on the job were Frank Martinez, Freddie Anderson, Adolf Wayne Bennion, Dee Lewis and Lyle Nichols. A couple of other workers were Gibb Rhodes and Art Kniesel who always seemed to keep a barrier between us. It probably took them to keep the Louie Welch outfit from turning into a fiasco at times when our horseplay almost took precedence over the job at hand.

This was also a time when hunting and fishing was the greatest. One time, Leo and I took my car, a 1941 Ford, and drove clear to the top of the Big Horn Mountains via Hyattville on a goat trail not fit for a jeep. Another time, we took about a twelve mile hike hunting deer from the top of Medicine Mountain to the foot of Hangover Trail. The only thing we shot at was a badger. Trips into Heart Lake were a yearly occurrence. One year, Louis Welch took his whole crew in and stayed four days. We had a whale of a time. We caught two 27 pound lake trout and a million smaller ones. The average was 2.5 to 3 pounds. The largest I caught personally was 7.25 pounds.

Top row: John and Helen; Leo and Dorothy Baird; front row: Jared and Elna

The little house we lived in then had only one bedroom, kitchen and living room so with a growing family, I had to build on two more rooms and completely rebuild the place. Leo and Frank helped me with quite a bit and it was transformed into a real nice home.

Linda was born March 4, 1949, in Powell, Wyoming. It was a thirty-mile drive and was almost a race against time. Twenty minutes after we arrived the baby was born. The nurse brought her out of the delivery room and said, "Here is your little pinky." She was quite red, but developed real well; really a beautiful child. She grew and developed quickly. She walked when she was eight months old and could carry on a conversation at eighteen months. She soon became a playmate for Kathleen.

Jared and Elna with Kathleen and Linda playing close by

Glenn and Lenore Lewis were very close to us, and their family and ours shared some interesting experiences. One special time was in the summer of 1948. Glenn and Lenore, Jay and Phyllis Partridge, Harold and VerJean Baker and Elna and I all got into Harold's old farm truck and headed for the Yellowstone National Park for a week-long outing. We traveled the beautiful Cook City Highway, and we stopped to camp wherever and whenever we chose. There were no regulations on campgrounds at that time. We enjoyed excellent fishing, and it seemed that the first equipment to be set up at a new campsite was the badminton set.

We had settled down almost to a routine of working and homemaking. I was ordained a Seventy by Spencer W. Kimball and was called to a stake mission. Elna was called to the Stake Primary Board and was very active in the M.I.A. as a counselor. The Lord blessed us in many ways. We bought a new car, a 1949 Pontiac.

Our first son, Robert Lewis Dickson was born October 2, 1950, in the Powell Hospital. He was quite thin and had a large misshaped nose. Everyone said he looked like Jimmy Durante, a popular comedian of the time. He grew and developed normally and became our chubbiest child. Then there were five of us. It sure took a lot of money to buy ice cream cones whenever we traveled somewhere in the car.

While working for Louis B. Welch, we were building a schoolhouse in Meteetse, Wyoming about sixty miles from home. We would come home only on weekends. It was summer and there was a lot of daylight after work. We would quite often go fishing after work as Meteetse is near the mountains where the Wood River and its many tributaries come out. There was excellent fishing.

I was walking along a trail alongside one of these streams when I saw a set of huge bear tracks in the soft mud. My mind went immediately to an occasion that happened two years before when a hunter, Ariel Walker, was presumed mauled by a grizzly bear. They had found some partial remains and his rifle with a full load of cartridges still in the magazine. One bullet had been fired, but the shell had not been ejected from the chamber. From where I stood, I could see a couple of good fishing holes. The timber was sparse and I assumed the bear had gone up the creek and into the timbers a quarter of a mile ahead. There was no sign of anything as far as I could see, so I kept on walking amazed at the size of those tracks.

There was a large bush growing on the side hill next to the trail with its branches hanging over the trail. I had just ducked under those branches when in a flash, I saw this big brown thing coming upon me. I screamed and slashed at it with my brand new bamboo fly rod. A beaver was up on the bank about eye level and I had startled it as I came around the bush. It made a quick dash for the water and the quickest way was right between my legs. For the next few minutes, I sat on the bank with a busted fly rod as hot and cold flashes ran up and down my spine. I was too scared to move. For an instant, I was sure that old grizzly bear had me. It seems funny now, but not then.

Things had become extremely slow in the job. We had just finished a schoolhouse in Meeteetse and one in Worland and winter was setting in. Welch cut his crew to only five of us and it became bitter cold, thirty-eight below zero. We had to build an addition on to the schoolhouse in Deaver, and we did all the excavations from under the existing building by hand, shoveling it out a ramp to the spoil pile.

When spring finally broke, Leo and I took the machinery up the North Fork of the Shoshone River and put in a diversion dam for a group of farmers. We hired three other fellows and spent about six weeks up there building a large head gate and intake for the canal to use for irrigation. Every night was spent fishing and sightseeing after work. One night, Leo and I counted one hundred and seventy five elk and eighty deer. It was early spring and the animals were still down in the lower winter range.

Once, Leo Baird and I took our pregnant wives and went on a fishing trip to Devil's Canyon. We were stopped on the road by an irate rider who threatened to kill us if we went any further. He was a shiftless bum and was dead drunk. Leo challenged him and he climbed off his horse and handed me the reins. When we saw that he had no gun and that he could hardly stand, I handed the bridle reins back to him and started the car. He said, "Dickson, you are okay, but that is more than I can say for this Harston S.O.B." Leo still wanted to punch him out for using such terrible language around our women, but it was probably more painful to just to leave him standing in the middle of the road, swearing as we drove away. Poor man got drunk and shot himself about six months later.

We drove on the rim of Devil's Canyon and camped there for the night. After cooking our supper and bedding down for the night, we had a very choice experience. The sky was so full of stars and seemed so close; it seemed we could almost reach out and touch them. The air was pure and warm. In the distance, we could see a few lights of home. We were so far above the noise and confusion of civilization that it seemed like heaven itself. At daylight the next morning, we descended to the bottom of Spider Leg Trail. The trail was so steep that we had to climb down a tree. We fished all day, stopping only to eat a nice lunch the ladies had prepared.

Late that evening, Leo and I stopped to clean our fish and sent the girls on up the trail. We were to catch up to them a few minutes later. When we left the creek and the noise of the stream we could hear the women calling, "Leo.....Jared!!!" To our dismay, we saw them high on the mountain side completely surrounded by rim rocks and a half mile from there the precipitous trail wound its way out of the canyon. They were afraid to come down to start over without our help. It was very dark when four tired people finally reached the car.

I finished remodeling our house in my spare time, and on the job we finished most of all the work Welch had in line. Leo and I were again sent away on a schoolhouse project over at Grass Creek, and with nothing else in mind, we began to look for greener pastures. About November 1, 1951, Leo and I caught the bus and again headed for Enumclaw. Uncle Owen had a big job going with a rock crusher and two sawmills. He had bought two new shovels since I had left and needed operators. We worked there until Thanksgiving and then flew home to get our families. We borrowed Mark Lewis' truck and the Bairds used Elmer Eyer's truck. Elmer and Rex drove the trucks and Leo and I drove the family cars. The move was very difficult. There was a lot of snow and it was very cold. At one icy pass in Montana, Elmer's truck skidded on the slick road and nearly went off a thousand foot embankment.

We found houses to rent and immediately went to work. I was running shovel and Leo worked in one of the mills.

Henry again came to the Northwest to work for Uncle Owen and the White River Lumber Co. He was a very skilled shovel operator and built many roads for White River. His family moved to Buckley where they raised most of their family. He was the branch president there.

We rented a little brown house out in the country and lived there until we could find a nice home and could handle it financially. We were living there when Dennis was born on June 2, 1952. I was sure pleased to have another boy. We think he was born with a chip on his shoulder because he was real hard to please, but he was probably one of the most fun kids we had because of his own mind sort of attitude.

Robert, Kathleen, Dennis and Linda

Work was fun. I ran the 22-B for a while and then spent about three months in the shop. Then I spent the rest of my time with Owen on the little truck crane. I enjoyed working on the fire trails, putting in culverts, cleaning up rock slides, etc. George Harding oiled for me. I did not like that proposition too well but tolerated it.

We got the word one day that Dad was having a bad time again. He had a bad heart for a long time and thought for a long time he was improving. In more testing they found that he had an ulcer that had partially healed and the scar tissue had built up so badly that there was not ample passageway to the small intestine. They operated and moved the stomach opening and the operation as such was successful, but his kidneys failed and he soon died.

Thelma and Katie came to his bedside as he slumped into a coma. He had oxygen tubes in his nose, but as all hopes were gone they removed the life-sustaining equipment. Then for the first time in several days, he spoke clearly and said, "I just want to go home. Is that too much to ask?" In a clear voice, he said, "Edna". His life faded, and he was gone. We believe Momma had come to see him home.

They held a funeral for him in Salt Lake City, and then his body was shipped to Cowley where we held another service. He was buried at Cowley at his plot alongside Momma's.

In May, 1952 we bought a nice home at 1453 Merrit Ave. in Enumclaw, Washington and we enjoyed a happy home for many years in this location.

In 1953, Owen's job with Weyerhaeuser ended and for a short time I was unemployed. We really capitalized on the situation. For the next several weeks we took our camping gear and all the kids and went on a super vacation, taking in a lot of state parks in Washington. Dennis was barely learning to walk, but Mom, Dad, and all the other kids enjoyed fishing, hiking and camping. We spent several days with Newell and Beth and their family down on the ocean beach.

Late in the summer, Henry and I started working for Uncle Lige. He had a large project at the Northern State Hospital that required a lot of demolition and site development for a new wing. He and I worked on this project for about six weeks. Henry was the foreman, and I was the crane operator. For the next eight years, I enjoyed operating machinery, being superintendent and learning the construction business in general.

April 3, 1954, Ellen was born. This year we spent the summer months in Toledo on a large rock crushing job. I ran a large dragline and put in many long hours. We rented a farmhouse and lived near the job. We rented our Enumclaw home to Paul and Janet Lee who were newlyweds. At Toledo, we planted a garden and had fruit trees. We enjoyed fishing and camping on weekends up at Spirit Lake at the base of Mt. St. Helens. On one occasion, Elna hooked a large harvest trout in the Cowlitz River and never forgave me for letting it get away.

After we finished the Toledo job, Elna and I took a few says off and went to the Olympic Peninsula for a short vacation. While on this trip we called home to see how the kids were doing and learned that Ron Brownell had been called as branch president of Buckley, and I was named the first counselor. I received my call the next Sunday. Elna was M.I.A. president and secretary of the Primary. Life was abundant and we enjoyed it.

Linda, Ellen, Jared, Elna and Kathy

Dennis and Robert

In 1955, Lige had a large contract to build the I-90 freeway through Snoqualmie Pass that took the larger part of three years to complete. My Uncle Lige was one of the largest contractors in Tacoma. It required changing the two-lane highway into four-lanes. My cousin Gwyn Dickson and I worked together a lot on this job. It was another season of long hours and hard work, but the monotony was broken by the challenge of running the 54-B and learning to operate the new LS-K-370, which were road construction equipment.

Several of us rented a summer home at Camp Mason and lived on the job during the week. At night after work, we would always fish for a while before dark. One particular day, we fished down the river for a couple of miles and I mentioned to Gwyn that we should be getting out of there before dark because we would not want to surprise a bear on the trail. His response was "Bears. I'm not afraid of bears."

We started up the trail. I was in the lead and had managed to get a few yards in front of him. When I was sure I was out of sight, I ducked behind a bush and waited for him to pass. He got a few steps ahead when I leaped on his back with a blood-curdling yell. His yell was more sincere and louder. If I could have held on it would have been a quick ride back to the pickup. I will always remember the fun times we had while on that job.

Another time on that job while fishing after work, Gwyn and I had caught a few fish and a huge salamander (water dog). We thought it would be fun to show our other roommates our catch. When we entered the cabin, Johnny Claybough was by the sink cleaning a bunch of fish he had caught. While he was working and talking, we secretly slipped the salamander in with his fish. He had it firmly in hand before he realized it was not a fish. I have never seen such a look of terror and surprise. He could not be convinced that he had caught the thing himself and vowed to get even.

Horseplay and practical jokes were the order of the day. My cousin Gwynn Dickson, Johnny Claybough, and others managed to keep things in an uproar. One day while we were doing some clearing the chainsaw broke down and that night I took it to the cabin to fix it. After supper when all had quieted down, I repaired the saw and started it up to make sure it was running properly. Well, Bobby Ganjidino had gone into the bathroom and was meditating half through his business when the saw started. Like a streak, he was out of the bathroom with his pants hanging on one foot as he shot through the living room where everyone was reading, and out the front door and into the front yard. There, standing in six inches of new snow, he got enough composure to yell, "What in the hell was that?"

Our routine was quite well set. I worked all week on the job and went home on weekends to work in and on the church. The next summer, I took the family to live in one of the cabins on the job during summer vacation. Mostly it was a very enjoyable time, but one time Ellen became too ill and we took her to the doctor in North Bend. Her fever rose to 106 degrees and the doctor worked feverishly over her for thirty minutes trying to get it down and into a normal condition. She healed rapidly and we knew our prayers had been answered.

We finished the job in 1957 and ended with a four-lane highway where it was only two lanes previously. We fought our way through thousands of cubic yards of solid rock, blue clay and at one point we had to divert the river channel. It was a fun job, and Lige had a feeling of pride to see it completed.

In 1958, we bought a home on Bonney Lake near Sumner and moved down there to be nearer the job. It was a neat multicolored brick home with radiant heat in the floor. It had a kitchen with glass all the way around it like the bridge on a ship. Elna just loved it there. She could watch the ducks and activity on the lake while doing the dishes. The children were growing and enjoying school, Primary and the fun of living in the country.

Jared, Newell, Henry and John

Jared, Elna & John, Helen's Kids in front row: Roy, Ellen,1959 Dennis, Vivian and Robert Back row: Linda, Doris, Kathy, Jack (John B) and Lynn

In the early part of 1959, I ran the big shovel most of the time and had many heart to heart talks with Lige. He was my ideal of what a Dickson Patriarch should be. He was large and energetic and his ability to work and succeed came second only to his devotion to his church work. At this time he was first counselor to the Stake President, but spent a lot of time as coordinator of the welfare in the region. He was respected both on and off the job. He gave me some good advice when he told me that if I worked as hard in my church work as I did at my personal business, that my personal business would be successful.

At this time our union went on a strike and it appeared it would be for a long time, and Lige had no alternative but to shut down.

Enumclaw Town League
John, Blain Nielsen, George Harding and Jared
Ed Smith, Paul Dickson and Leo Baird

1960

John and Henry were working for Uncle Owen who was building a road up above Darrington, Washington. Having nothing else to do, I went up there to see what was going on. Weyerhauser Lumber Co. bought the White River Co. and Owen's job with them soon ended. Henry worked with Owen until Owen quit the business and sold a lot of his equipment and business to John and Henry. I also bought one of Owen's power shovels. We traded our Enumclaw house for a 22-B shovel that Owen owned and this started us out in the heavy construction business. We worked together for a couple of years.

I have to reflect back at times and evaluate my judgment. The situation was this: I had a good job that probably paid better than most, a beautiful home, five lovely children who were all in grade school, and Elna and I were both entrenched in church work. Times were good, and it would seem that I may have been a little too impulsive to uproot all this and start something new a long way from home. It turned out that we made an excellent choice. The church needed us in Arlington. The income was better and the opportunities far outweighed what we were accustomed to.

Henry was the first to move to Granite Falls where he bought a big house where he could raise a large garden and the rest of his family. John and I followed later to establish our homes. John ran into financial difficulty when a contractor refused to pay him for a rock crushing job and the decision was made to sell the crusher and other equipment to Summit Timber and go to work for them. John, Henry and Joe all worked for Summit Timber. I started a business of my own.

We first moved to a little summer cabin located about four miles north of Granite Falls on Canyon Creek. It was a rustic type log cabin with all the modern conveniences and was well landscaped. We lived there for a year and a half, but we knew we wanted a better home and better opportunities for the kids.

## Granite Falls House

We got the scare of our lives one day. We were on our way to Everett and taking Linda to school. We stopped at the end of our driveway and sent Linda across the highway to get the mail from our mailbox. A large logging truck came roaring down the highway. Linda waited for it to go by and then stepped out onto the highway behind it. Linda did not see the truck approaching from the other direction. The truck swerved to avoid hitting her and she stepped back just in time to avoid a terrible accident. That gave both Elna and I nightmares.

Most of our experiences while living there were good. Robert and Dennis had their bedroom in a detached utility room while the girls slept upstairs. It was more of a loft than a bedroom. The house was heated by electricity, but for economics, I put in a wood heater. This made chores for the boys because I would fell alder and maple trees on the property and split them into stove-wood lengths. The boys would haul it up to the house in their little wagon. I didn't know until many years later that half of the firewood went into the river instead of the chore wagon.

Dennis had a rabbit named "Old Thumper" and Kathleen laid claim to an old resident tomcat she named "Smokey". Smokey was later killed by a tomcat or bobcat after a high-speed chase around the yard.

Dennis and Kristy with dog, Spunky

Dennis' dog, Spunky

We looked for a house to rent in Arlington and after several weeks decided it was impossible to find what we wanted so we looked into the possibility of buying a home. A nice brick house on East 5th Street was available so we bought it. At the time, it seemed awfully high at $16,800, but we really liked it. That fall the kids started school and we found it very convenient for them to walk to all functions.

Elna, Jared and Spunky in front of Arlington home

January 13, 1962, Kristine was born, but not without some difficulty. That night in the waiting room seemed like an eternity. Elna went into labor as was normal with all the other children and after the appropriate time, I heard the baby cry. It must have been thirty minutes later that Dr. Huber came out and said, "I'm sorry, I failed." It flashed through my mind that something had happened to Elna, and then he said, "I didn't get you a boy". I was relieved and actually did not consider it a failure at all.

This year I took my first big job as a contractor. I bid and succeeded in getting a job wrecking a large warehouse in Bellingham.

We learned again that you do not have to be dead to enjoy heaven. We had a brand new home, a new job, and a brand new baby. Our family was now complete and we enjoyed life to the fullest.

In church work, I was called to be M.I.A. Superintendent as well as being the scoutmaster. I organized the first B.S.A. unit in Arlington

Ward. It started with five members called a neighborhood patrol and within a year we chartered the first Boy Scout Troop #212. Elna was called to be the M.I.A. President. We worked together for a couple of years.

On the job, I worked for loggers with the little shovel (22-B) and then in the fall I took on a large road building project for Pope and Talbot near Skykomish. John and I had looked at the job and decided to bid it. I did it under the Robert Dickson Company and he would help me on a rental lease, but I ended up doing 90% of the job. We had a lot of good experiences. Our crew consisted of Jack Dickson, Jerry Dearinger and Chuck Blankenship. Others helped out occasionally. I bought a new D7 caterpillar and air trac and compressor.

It was on this job that Jack started complaining about his right arm hurting. We never took it seriously because he always seemed to get the best of a wrestling match or other horseplay that went on every day. As time went on the hurt got worse until one night he and Leo went bowling and it hurt so bad he went to a doctor. In a few days and a good many tests, it was proven that he had cancer of the bone and it became necessary to amputate his arm above the elbow to save his life. He had received his mission call, but this had to be postponed for a year.

In this year, we also started building the new church house in Arlington. Bob Jones, then a counselor in the Branch Presidency, practically performed a miracle in persuading the brethren in Salt Lake City to let us build such a structure. We were very small in numbers, but strong in the priesthood and had a determination to do the Lord's work. A building superintendent, Lynn McCardel, was called and with donated labor we built the first three stages in about two years. This changed our lifestyle somewhat being that we had to schedule work parties every other day and on Saturdays.

It was a healthy time in our ward as far as enthusiasm and participation were concerned. John followed Knud Swensen as branch president, and I was called as Priest Quorum advisor. This job I held for many years and had many choice experiences with a lot of fine young men. I am still proud of men like Gary and Darrel Jones, Wally Baird, Graham Swensen, Ken and Dick Simkins, Robert and Dennis Dickson, Jerry and Tom Dearinger, Phil Sprague, Duane Eyre, Steve Symmes, Darrel and Don Motes, and Mark Lemon and others who have each played a very important part in my life.

Here's an analogy I wrote of my experience as a Priest Quorum Advisor.

*Building Men is Like Building A Road, by Jared Dickson*

*A road building contractor who worked mostly on US Forest Service contracts was called affectionately "Mister Jarrard" by some of his crew. Mr. Jarrard's day would begin at five a.m. After morning prayer and breakfast with his wife, Elna, he would get in the crew bus and head for work. As he left home, his six children would still be asleep.*

*His first stop was to pick up Jack who lived in a big white house on the banks of the Stillaguamish River. Jack was eighteen years old and came to Mr. Jarrad's job to run a brand new D7E caterpillar tractor his Dad, John, had bought to go with his contracting business. Jack had had a little experience on his Dad's jobs, but with the new cat, he very soon became a very skilled operator.*

*The next stop was to pick up Joe. Joe was seventeen, large for his age, and a very husky young man. He was an apprentice on the machinery but soon became very efficient.*

*The next stop was to pick up Jerry. Jerry was eighteen and was just out of high school where he was a star athlete in baseball and basketball. He learned quickly to drive a dump truck and to run the air tract rock drill.*

*Mr. Jarrard was the priest quorum advisor and the boys were priests. The boys were working for the summer to earn money to go on their missions.*

*The boys were the best of friends all working for the same purpose. It was easy for them to discuss Sunday lessons or learn their missionary discussions as they rode in the crew bus. They all had a very keen sense of humor and at times levity had to be restrained. D&C 21 "Many are cold, but few are frozen." It was usually a wrestle to see who would ride in the backseat or who would ride shotgun to keep the driver awake.*

*On the job it was all work, packing powder, shooting stumps, hooking chokers, yarding logs, etc. At one spot on a steep side hill, a big rock had to be removed. It was about three feet in diameter and half of it was above grade. When it came out, a stream of ice cold water gushed out and it was immediately called "The Moses Rock". A small culvert was installed to carry the water across the road and it continued to drain about five gallons per minute. It probably still does. It was a Godsend on a hot summer day to stop and be refreshed. Sometimes the whole crew would gather at the Moses Rock to rest a few minutes and fill their thermoses. Someone mentioned the spring is like the gospel. It is there for the taking, no matter how often repeated it is still refreshing.*

*These special times with the boys happened during the summers of 1962, 1963 and 1964. It is now 2008 and what has happened since 1962 is the rest of the story. From this group came bishops, stake presidents, and a General Authority.*

*Watching Jack (John B. Dickson) speak in General Conference as a General Authority*

In 1963, the work on the church house continued, and life at home was busy and fun. Kathy and Linda took on a large paper route in the country and we got a new Volkswagen bug after the wheels were literally run off the Rambler station wagon. There were many interesting experiences…Linda ran over a family dog and killed it. All the members cried, including the father. Vivian, Linda's cousin, was doing the paper route one night when she hit a bear with the Volkswagen and did considerable damage. One time Kathy surprised an eagle eating a rabbit along the side of the road. As she approached, the eagle took off carrying the rabbit with him. At about fifty feet, he dropped the rabbit and it came crashing through the windshield. One night, Elna was helping with the route using the family car. Kathy went on her half and when completed she started looking for Mom. It was way out on a country road on a blind corner when she finally ran into Mom and bent the fenders.

This year Leo and his family moved to Washington and came to work for us. We had a lot of fun up on the Johnson Creek job. We stayed in a little trailer house. There was hardly any winter that year and consequently had very little time off.

In 1964, the Cascade Stake was formed. Robert E. Jones was called as the Stake President. He chose Elna as Primary President and I was a high counselor. Elna held her position for eight years and did an excellent job. She was a terrific organizer and knew how to get the job done.

During this time, our children were growing and it was becoming more fun to go on trips to the mountains, etc. We bought a 1962 Oldsmobile station wagon especially to hold our growing family and to pull our little trailer house. We took it as far as Wyoming once. One particular time while on that trip, the muffler fell off from our car and we pulled into a little roadside park to fix it. While there, Robert and Dennis pulled out their fishing poles and immediately started catching fish out of the river. Elna was looking on as other fishermen landed their boat nearby. She admired their catch of fish and we were all surprised to see her end up with all their fish. That made the men legal to fish some more and we had a nice meal.

In 1965, Elna and I had always talked about and planned to build an estate so that someday we would become financially independent.

After prayerful consideration and advice from Uncle Lige, we decided to invest in some gravel land. We had to cash out our life insurance policies and remortgage our home to get the necessary cash to set up business.

This year we built the Diamond Road (2.5 miles long) for the Everett Lumber Company. We bought a new one yard shovel-LS-98 that proved to be a real asset for many years. We finished this job in good time and enjoyed the new machinery and a good crew. Chuck VanBelle, Jerry Dearinger, Dave Wright, and several others did a good job. Herb York came to work for us near the end of this job.

We had some good experiences while Elna worked in the Stake Primary presidency. In 1965, I drove her and her counselors to Salt Lake City for a Primary conference. It was a very spiritual occasion culminated by a large refreshment session in the Salt Palace where all husbands were invited. We enjoyed visits from the general authorities in our home and in every way we tried to magnify our callings and were blessed for the effort.

In 1966, we got a huge contract building the Tupsoo Pass, Meadow Mountain road and also the Upper South Fork and Upper Canyon. We used the same crew and machinery except that John came to help when he finished the job he was working on. He brought his equipment and crew. It was on this job that John lost his eye while changing a battery on his caterpillar.

Ken Johnson appeared for the Christmas holidays and favorably impressed the family.

They were married June 23, 1967.

In 1967 Linda graduated from Arlington High School as one of the best ten grade point average students in the class. This achievement earned her a scholarship to Brigham Young University. All the girls worked hard on their paper route and driving truck for the cannery in order to pay for their college.

Robert graduated in 1968 from high school. He was voted best actor of the year for his efforts in "Barefoot in the Park."

Elna worked hard and diligently in her many duties as a wife and mother, my full-time secretary and bookkeeper, stake Primary president, and found time on Sundays to be with me on High Council assignments.

Robert left on his mission to England in November, 1969. It was very cold and he got off to a real bad start. He was put with a very lazy companion and the weather was extremely damp and cold. His letters for the first few months were very discouraging, but with faith and good works, he filled a bright and successful mission.

During this time, we began to see a little financial gain. We sold half of the gravel pit for more than we paid for the whole thing. We applied this money to another piece of property known as the Lee property and after partially clearing it, we sold it for three times the purchase price.

Linda was attending Brigham Young University and chose to spend one semester at the Church college of Hawaii. She returned to B.Y.U. and soon afterwards struck up an acquaintance with a bright young, clean-cut fellow named Gary Jones from a town close to Arlington. A short time later they were married and we were more than pleased to include him in our family.

Jared and Elna, Linda and Gary, Audrey and Robert (Bob) Jones

Dennis graduated from high school in 1970. At this age he became quite rebellious. I am sure he led a good life and had good friends, but he didn't always conduct himself as his parents wished. One of his good friends was Randy Williams. This year he and Ellen had parts in the school play "Oklahoma." Ellen had one of the lead parts.

It was early spring when I had a job with Buse Lumber to haul right of way logs and cedar poles to the Sultan Basin. It was while working here that I was involved in an accident that sent me to the hospital with three broken ribs and a punctured lung. I spent the next seven days in the hospital and six weeks at home recovering. When I recovered enough to travel, we took a nice trip to Utah and Wyoming. I had to be very careful and did not get to fish very much, but we did enjoy the trip.

We had a Forest Service contract to demolish an old country bridge on the South Fork of the Stillaguamish River near Verlot. It worked out very well because of a fire shut-down in the woods. I got some good help from Ken Johnson, Joe Dickson, Frank Baird and Dennis. It was a good job and a lot of fun.

Dennis was lighting up the outdoor barbecue using gasoline and was accidently burned over most of his body. The burns were only superficial and left no scars due to Kathy quickly running the garden hose over him, but it was a very painful experience. It scared Elna quite badly as she could not stand to see him in such agony. Perhaps the Lord had to teach him a little humility before leaving on his mission in a few days. When we took Dennis to the mission home, Robert had just returned from his mission and he drove to Utah with us to enter Brigham Young University. This was a special time in our lives.

That night in Wayne and Veloy Hansen's home, the boys came to ask for the car. They both had snow on their shoulders and looked tall and handsome. Their mother and I could not have been prouder. The feeling of being blessed was very vivid by the fact that only two days before my brother Newell's boy, Lloyd, was buried in Twin Falls. He was only fifteen years old and was a very good looking young man who had all the qualities that my boys had. He was killed in an automobile accident while out riding with some of his friends.

Ellen graduated from Arlington High School in 1972 and received many honors. She was cheerleader the last two years in school. That summer she drove truck for the canning factory to earn money for college. That fall she and Robert entered B.Y.U. We gave them the 1970 Montego for transportation. Robert had worked in the woods for Summit Timber to earn money for his school.

Dennis returned home from his mission to Hawaii in 1973 with a whole new concept of life. He was determined to succeed in getting an education and bettering his life. He worked with me on the roads for Summit Timber Company that summer. Some of the roads we built for Summit were Pow Wow, Spot Slowdown, Big Foot, Helena Ridge, North Mountain, Swarty Lake, Good Murph, Sun Burst, Black Trail, No Option and Lower Mid. We also built roads for the state of Washington and Menasha. We also did a lot of non-contracted work.

One time while the operating engineers (a union) were out on strike, Gwynn Dickson came out and ran the LS-98 crane for us. He and Randy Williams worked up on Murphy Ridge.

## Gwynn Dickson, cousin

I was building a road for Cliff Toungate on the Lower Pilchuck. It was in the late fall when the deer hunting season was open. I always carried my rifle in the pickup in hopes of seeing a deer on the job or on the road going to and from the work site.

One particular day, I quit work a little early and took my rifle and scooted up and around a heavy patch of timber. I saw a lot of tracks, but no deer. I hunted until nearly dark and then decided I had better get back to the truck while it was still light. The hillside was quite steep and I found that I could hold the gun in front of me and squat down on my heels and go sliding. This worked great until I came to a place that began to be a little steeper and I was going too fast for comfort. I grabbed and held on to a small tree that stopped by descent. I planned to keep going as I was making good time and it was kind of fun. When I tried to get started again, I found I could not let go of the little tree. It was as if my hand had frozen shut and I could not open it. When I got to my feet, I could see a sudden drop off only a few feet in front of me. I went around to the side and as I looked back I could see a straight cliff of about fifty feet with nothing but huge broken boulders at the bottom. I am so grateful for the hand of providence that has been shown me throughout my life. It was not just by coincidence that the little tree was there to stop me. The Lord truly cares for us personally.

Elna was released from the Stake Primary after spending eight years of a very fruitful experience. She was immediately called to serve in the Young Women's M.I.A. presidency. In 1975, the stake presidency was released and also five of the high counselors. I was one of those released. I was the only one of the original twelve high counselors to serve the complete tenure of the stake presidency. I had served for twelve years and look back on this experience as one of the best in my life. When I was doing the best of my ability in church work, we prospered both financially and in seeing the church programs change the lives of people. I am extremely grateful for knowing and having the influence of these great men in my life.

Robert married Jennifer Gray in the Salt Lake City temple, November 1, 1974.

April 18, 1975 started out to be the greatest time of our lives. Elna and I were on a trip to Provo to see Robert graduate from B.Y.U. We had a wonderful time planned. Mark and Charlotte were bringing down a load of meat, Ellen was there, Rex and Cathy were being married so Glenn and Lenore had come for the occasion. We were happy, in love, and better off financially than we had ever been in our lives. It seemed we were sitting on top of the world.

It was quite a shock to us to learn that Elroy, Elna's brother, was in the hospital and had a malignant tumor removed from his leg. The real shock came later that night after everyone had visited and enjoyed the evening. Elna was taking a shower when she came rushing in the bedroom where I was and said, "You know, I am really concerned. I have a lump in my breast as large as an egg". This started the nightmare that lasted two and a half years. The very thought of cancer is terrible, but the step by step course that we took seemed worse as it went along.

We never told anyone in Utah the real reason we cut our visit short. We dashed home to our family doctor in Arlington, Dr. Huber. He sent Elna down to Seattle for x-rays and this confirmed our dreaded thoughts of cancer. Dr. Huber came over to our house at 11:00 pm to give us the bad news. The next morning Elna was admitted to the Veterans Affairs Hospital in Seattle. Several days were spent taking tests and consultations and more tests until the doctors finally chose to operate. She was given a radical mastectomy which took her entire left breast, all the muscles and lymph nodes from under her arm. I thanked the Lord the operation was successful.

From this time on our lifestyle was changed to include tests, treatments, and a million doctor appointments. She underwent all kinds of treatments to include cobalt radiation, chemotherapy, and special diets. For a time, it seemed she was getting better and we were even optimistic of a cure, but our hopes were only short lived when they discovered cancer cells in her bone marrow. I was told then that her life expectancy was less than a year. I probably made a mistake in trying to harbor this information to myself. I tried in every way to make her remaining year as normal as possible. In doing this, I had to tell people she was doing fine.

It was a very difficult time. The kids did not appreciate how sick she really was because they did not know. Our friends left us alone, probably thinking that Elna would not enjoy company or an evening out or anything we were accustomed to doing with friends. It was hard to keep things on an even plane when everyone deserted us. Even Linda and Gary went for nearly a year without inviting us out or even coming to see us on Sundays. They probably thought the little children would annoy Elna. If they only knew how much she loved them and that staying away only added to her grief. I cannot explain all the anguish I went through, considering my life without her, making funeral arrangements in my mind, trying to tend to business and all the time trying to pretend everything was normal. I did a lot of praying and gathered a great deal of strength from my testimony of the gospel. Life would have been impossible without this inner strength.

In 1976, we completed the work on Helena Ridge and North Mountain for Summit. We also started the Swartz Lake job. Gary talked me into buying a new truck, 1975 IHC H200, and this proved to be a large step forward. We also hired Cliff Staylen who was one of our greatest assets. He is a fine gentleman who knew how to run all kinds of equipment. Most of all, he knew how to get things done. He hauled rock on our jobs and did a lot of work for Summit Timber.

We had some misfortune with two of our old Ford dump trucks. Dennis was driving the first. We were doing some clearing on Murphy Ridge and hauling the debris from the roadside. I would load his truck with the crane and he would haul it down a steep road to a large burn bay about a quarter of a mile away. This time, his truck jumped out of gear and there was not enough air to activate the air brakes. He plummeted down the steep grade, through the burn bay area and over a ten-foot berm of crushed rock and sailed thirty feet through the air and crashed into a field of logging slash. I hurried to my pickup and drove down to the scene and found Dennis lying on the floorboards unconscious. I quickly gave him a blessing and went for help. I got the help I needed from a G & D logging unit nearby and I also called for an ambulance on their radio. We rushed him to the Darrington Clinic for emergency treatment and then on to the Arlington Hospital. By the time we got to Arlington he was semi-conscious but very incoherent. He recovered quickly from a mild concussion and a very sore arm. It could have been much worse.

G and D logging Crew

Only a few days later Allen Baker jumped into a truck and kicked it out of gear without building sufficient air pressure. It had no emergency brakes and was headed directly over a seventy foot cliff. I saw the truck disappear over the ledge and ran to the edge to see that it had run straddle a large windfall log lying against the cliff and it had slid the length of it, remaining upright. A pole had gone through the windshield and on through the back of the cab, missing Allen's head by inches. He was lucky to be unhurt.

In October, Elna and I went on a real nice vacation trip that took us to Provo where Elna got to see all her family. Ellen was still at school and she took us to meet Marvin Slovacek whom she later married. He is a very good looking young man.

Ellen and Marvin Slovacek

From Provo, we drove on south to the North Rim of Grand Canyon and enjoyed the view. Being so late in the year, all the tourist facilities were closed. From there we took in Bryce Canyon and then on down through Zion Canyon National Park. That scenery is something out of this world. We spent the night in St. George and visited with the Simkins. Probably the highlight of the whole trip was a visit to Crater Lake in Oregon. That is one beautiful place. This was the last trip that Elna could really enjoy. We thanked the Lord for this wonderful experience.

In the spring around Memorial Day, Elna, Kristy and I were invited to go with the Jones up to the 108-mile house in British Columbia. We took the pickup and boat and were all set for a nice time, but Elna's health worsened. She felt rotten and had a nose bleed almost continuously. I felt guilty leaving her long enough to go fishing.

Dennis married a beautiful girl, Dawn Stanley, in July of 1975 in the Hawaii temple. It was really wonderful to Dennis to be able to be married where he served his mission.

In July of 1977, Gary showed real concern for Elna and it brought out a part of him I had never known. He suggested that he and I go to Mexico and check out the Canteras Clinic for cancer. This we did and were impressed to have Elna admitted there for treatment. She stayed there for three weeks and left feeling much improved. Her improvement was only short lived. Back home she was given a room at the Veteran's Hospital and had permanent residency there, although she was allowed to come home for a few days occasionally. Her last trip to the hospital I had to carry her to the car because it hurt too bad to walk. At the car, she had me stop while she had a long look at the house and yards. I could tell that she felt she would never see her home again.

1977

Left to right: Robert, Jennifer and Brock; Kathy, Ken and Jonathan, Aaron, David; Dennis, Dawn and Michael; Jared, Elna and Dani; Ellen, Marv; Kristy; Linda, Gary and Trista, Shawna, Carrie, Brooke

September 20, 1977, Elna passed away at 10:20 pm. I was alone with her the last few hours and in no way can I express what I felt, so I will not try. There has never been a greater love than what we shared for each other.

After the funeral, the boys took me on a fishing trip to Lake Moccasin and Lake Chipaca for a few days. It was a good gesture, and I appreciated it. The real letdown came around Christmas time and her birthday. I became very discouraged and lonely.

Dennis ready to fish

I tried hard to make a happy home for Kristy. She was going to Arlington High School and early morning seminary. I would get up and fix breakfast and would try to be home soon after she got home from school. She helped me pick out a new pickup truck and new Datsun car. She was discouraged and saddened by the loss of her mother, but I was proud of the way she stood up to the pressure.

In the early spring of 1978, I had a lot of work near town and I had more work to do than I could handle with the job and household chores. I was so discouraged with the breakdowns and hassle with inheritance tax. It seemed that every way I turned, there was a mountain too high to climb. Nothing was fun. I seemed like a misfit although some of my friends tried to include me in some of their activities.

# MARIE

Things started to change when I hired Marie Spletter to come and cook the evening meal. I found her to be a very delightful person to know. She is an excellent cook and seemed to be genuinely interested in our home and family. After dinner each day I found her very interesting to talk to. I would take her on short drives and show her some of my construction projects. As we talked and got better acquainted, I found we had a great deal in common. She loved to hike, hunt and fish and the out of doors. I am not sure of the exact moment I began to fall in love with her, but it seemed that suddenly there was an urgency to have her as my wife.

It seemed quite soon after Elna's passing, but all reason, and I believe inspiration from God, told me I was doing the right thing. When I proposed to her I found that she had had the same impressions. We set a date and were married July 7, 1978, in the Ogden Temple. Most of our children and a lot of our friends were there to see us sealed for time and eternity.

Mike and Patty Bryant, Marie and Jared, Linda Erickson, Laurie
Swallows

Gary, Linda, Kristy, Marie, Jared, Ellen, Dennis, Dawn

A three week honeymoon followed and was one of the most fun times of my life. We camped on Grey's River and had a bath in a cold stream. Wow! We had a great experience fishing on Yellowstone Lake and in Devil's Canyon. We stayed up on top of the Big Horn Mountains and had a special evening with Henry and Geneva's family at their family reunion at the Porky Pine Campground. We fished in the Tongue River and several other creeks. We had a good visit with my brother, Earl and Margaret, and with Mark and Glenn and their families.

The hikes, the fishing and visits were all great, but the climax of the whole trip was when only ten miles from the trail we decided to hike into Deep Lake. We were not too well prepared, but we did have one pack board. I carried the sleeping bags and Marie carried the creel. We had salt, a half-pound of bacon and three green peppers. Not much for a three day trip, but we had confidence in catching fish. It took us seven hours to hike in, but was well worth it. We caught all we could eat and on the second day we loaded up with our limit and prepared to hike out. There was an abundance of snow in drifts along the way to preserve our catch until we reached the truck and ice box.

At home we found everything in good shape. I had Dave Parshall hired to help Kristy and he had the yards in fine shape for our open house reception on July 27th. Cliff Staylen kept the truck running and cared for all the other business obligations while we were gone.

Robert and Jennifer and family moved out from Utah to help me with the business. He was of considerable help to me in estate planning and helping me to straighten out our inheritance tax and financial matters. We formed a corporation (Arlanco Inc.) to carry out the business I had done previously as the Robert J. Dickson Company. We transferred a lot of the assets to the new corporation. This made me owner of all the stock in Arlanco. Robert had the opportunity of buying stock and thus becoming a part owner of the corporation.

I was called to be High Priest group leader in 1979. Marie was the Laurel leader in the ward. Kristine graduated from Arlington High School and because her ACT tests had been lost, it was necessary for her to begin the summer term at Brigham Young University in order to qualify for entrance in the fall. This gave her time to adjust to the big school and it was good for her.

At home things were fine. We raised a fair garden and Marie was busy doing all that needed to be done at home and took care of her sick sister-in-law, Pat Evans.

This year we completed the Sun Burst and Black Trail roads and were successful bidding on No Option. Marie and I stayed close to the job, taking only a few days off. We had no vacation as such.

December 11, 1979, Darcy Ellen was born, the fifth daughter of Gary and Linda. Linda had considerable trouble at childbirth. Her uterus had a hole in it that bled profusely. She lost so much blood that she lost consciousness. Only the quick attention of the hospital team and the help of the Lord saved her life.

In 1980 we were very busy on the roads. We completed No Option, Dan's Creek and Markworth jobs and also started the Menasha Road. Marie and I took the little trailer to the Marksworth job and spent a lot of time there. We found a thousand acres of chanterelle mushrooms and hike and fished a lot.

During our annual downtime in 1981, Marie and I went on a trip to Mexico where Jack and Delores and family were presiding over the Mexico City North Mission for the church. We spent nine days with them touring the country and visiting the many shops, theaters and museums. It was fun and we learned a lot. From there we came back to southern California and enjoyed the sun. We drove to St. George and visited with Rex and Norma Eyre. I had not seen Rex for nine years. He was my best friend during high school days.

We were able to send Kristy on a B.Y.U. semester abroad tour. It was a family effort to save and plan for this occasion and I am sure she appreciated it. She toured most of the European continent, including a trip to Israel.

At work we finished the Menasha Road and started the Lower Mid. We learned something new in road building when we leased a FMC 3400 and discovered we could build more road in adverse conditions than by any other means we had used previously. We got along so well that we finished the job a year ahead of schedule. By October 1, 1981 we finished all our projects and moved our machinery to the shop for repair. We built the Stillaguamish Athletic Club that opened July 1, 1982.

Rob and his wife, Beth

Marie spent a lot of time tending young mothers in the family. This year babies were born to Laurie Swallows, Patty Bryant, Terry Zaug, and Linda Erickson. Ellen was expecting her third before the end of the year. Marie spent a couple of weeks with each of them. Kathy was expecting her sixth.

I went to Alaska with Marie to see the Erickson's new arrival. They were building a new house and we got there in time to help put on the finishing touches and get them moved in in time for Thanksgiving. We drove about one hundred miles up towards the interior from Anchorage. We saw a few moose and a lot of snow. Saturday we are scheduled to go on a sightseeing tour.

1982 was a good year for us. Our family consisted of Marie and I and Kristy. Honorary members were Old Trooper (the dog), Wincellas (the cat), and Puppy (Kristy's dog). Trooper was a purebred German Shorthair hunting dog that was too ugly to be registered with the rest of her litter. In spite of her unorthodox pace and seemingly retarded actions, she was a good hunter and gave us lots of enjoyment on the frequent hunting trips to eastern Washington. Old Puppy was a male Chinese Pug and came at a time when Kristy needed a true friend. He was cute but had a real equilibrium problem. He was the only dog I knew that had to lean on the fire hydrant in order to lift his leg. Old Wincellas, the cat, came to our doorstep as an undernourished three week old kitten. Kristy quickly took him in, fed him and gave him a dignified name. All this attention went to his head as he thought he owned the place.

Kristy and Larry Tate were married in the Seattle Temple and sealed for eternity in a very spiritual ceremony conducted by her uncle, John Dickson. It seemed special to me as I felt that Elna was there. This was confirmed to me by Ellen and Kathy who also felt her presence. We were all very impressed with what a fine young man Larry is. I am sure they were brought together by the spirit of God.

On the job all was going good. We completed several big road jobs and had the equipment and personnel to make things work. Robert did an excellent job setting up the books. The new computer helped us a lot in estimating and accounting. What I thought was another big asset was that Jack and Delores and family came home from Mexico where he had been serving as mission president. He would be over the logging and construction. Things couldn't be better for Arlanco.

This year we bought twelve acres near Prospect Point and built a new shop on it and were just in the process of building it and repairing machinery when the subject of Adam-ondi-ahman came up. Graham Doxey and Elder Adams came to our house to interview prospective missionaries for the Adam-ondi-ahman project. Marie and I were very excited and it took very little salesmanship to convince us to go on an eighteen month mission for the church. We trusted the business was in good hands with Robert and Cliff and that we would let the missionaries live in our house. It seemed that nothing could go wrong, and it would be a great experience for us. So we dedicated a year and a half to the Lord's work and gladly accepted the call.

In April of 1983, we bought a new Ford Ranger pickup, rented a U-Haul trailer, loaded up the necessities and headed for Missouri. I complained about pulling a trailer until I was reminded that it beat a handcart. After that we felt blessed in all respects.

We stopped for a couple of days in Wyoming to visit friends and relatives. While there we borrowed my brother Earl's pickup and drove up into the foothills of Pryor Mountain and tried to find the place I had

had a spiritual experience with a horse many years before. We actually found the spot where the horse had been stuck in the rocks and found where we had started a fire forty-two years before to get warm after I had been injured. I knelt in the same spot I did long ago and felt the same spirit I did then. Marie also got a strong witness of the spirit.

We drove on toward Missouri, across Wyoming and stayed in North Platte for the night. We followed a big storm across the plains and although the driving conditions were not that bad for us, we saw where the snowplows had piled up huge drifts of snow only hours ahead of us. The next day we rolled on into Missouri. We were impressed with the thousands of snow geese we saw at a game refuge as we left Nebraska. We stayed at a motel in Cameron, Missouri, only a few miles from Adam-ondi-ahman and the next day we had arrived with great anticipation determined to do our very best in the work that was to be done. We were one of eleven couples sent there.

Marie, Earl, Margaret Dickson

John H., Helen Dickson

Darren, Fayetta Johnson with kids, Jared, Elder and Sister Richards

Elder Dean Bair was the project leader. He and his wife, Dorothy, were from Ephrata, Washington, and were on a mission in Arizona when called to come and direct the project at Adam-ondi-ahman. I admired his hard work and leadership ability.

Our first assignment was to locate and acquire the machinery necessary to clear the land and get rid of the Thorny Black Locust that had infected the land. Marie and I traveled the better part of four states looking for the best deal on a half yard crane and a D6-C caterpillar. We found the machinery we like and recommended it to Elder Doxey and Bishop Peterson. They, in turn, went through the formal acquisition process and brought me checks. We bought the LS-58 Linkbelt crane locally and I sold my own D6-C to the church, which was mostly a donation, and had it moved from Washington to Missouri.

By May 30, 1983, we had all the machinery and crew to do the job we had been sent there to do. The crew consisted of Elder Bair and Dorothy, Boyd Butler and Myrtle, Chad and Nora Burbidge, Adrian and Vivian Richins, John (the brother of Jared) and Helen Dickson, Harley and Shirley Lythgoe, Eric and Joni Christianson, David and Michelle Richards, Darren and Fayetta Johnson, with Carlos, Nancy, Frank and Darwin (their foster children), Paul and Vera Adams, Lisa Patch and her husband, Alec and Nyda Allen, and Marie and I. Later came Elders Pace, Brinkerhoff and Reed. Elder Green was there only for a short period but had to leave because of Sister Green's allergies.

We worked long hours of hard work and accomplished a lot. Besides the logging, we maintained and built roads and fences, continued the cleanup of old houses and dump sites, built over four miles of new roads that permitted better access to the valley and helped with drainage runoff. We built new ponds and cleaned others for erosion control. We cleared over 400 acres of Thorny Locust trees and reclaimed the land for pasture. We built a fourplex apartment house for the missionaries to live in and remodeled older farmhouses for the same purpose. Mostly for all that worked there, they realized a great satisfaction just to be part of it. Others, I am sorry to say, did it for their own glory and gratification and failed to reap all the spiritual growth they could have attained.

We enjoyed the birthdays and all other occasions we could think of to hold a potluck or planned party to play horseshoes, square dance or just to sing and enjoy each other's company. We held our own study meetings twice a week and went to Trenton on Sundays. They had an organized branch of the church there where we all had a chance to participate.

We were thrilled to have a lot of our family come to visit us. Gary and Linda and family came first and stayed several days. Then Ken and Kathy and their family came. Ellen drove all the way from Texas with her children to spend a few days. It sure seemed good to see all the grandchildren David Johnson, son of Kathy and Ken, was eight years old and wanted to come to Adam-ondi-ahman to be baptized by his grandfather. In preparation for this, Marie and I had

found a little pool of clear water in a little canyon just west of Springhill. The preceding rains had washed the rocks clean. A little year-round stream furnished water for the pool which was about ten feet in diameter and approximately four to five feet deep. The rocks and surrounding hills made it perfect for the congregation of missionaries and families. We sang, Elder Doxey gave the opening prayer, my brother John gave a very inspirational talk and I baptized David. His father, Ken, gave him the confirmation and blessing. It was a very spiritual occasion.

We declared a fifteen-day holiday on the way home and came via Montana and Wyoming. Fishing in Devil's Canyon was good and it was good to see Laurie and Steve and family. We fished and went on a couple of outings with them. Then on to Leavenworth and home via Steven's Pass. All the colors of Tumwater Canyon and Index Mountain were beautiful.

I cannot describe the chaos we found at home. The garden and fruit trees were completely overgrown with blackberries, the carport had blown down in a previous windstorm and was never rebuilt, the basement had flooded and was never completely drained. All the carpets and walls were rotted and covered with mildew. It took us weeks to dispose of all the contaminated furnishings and dry out and clean up everything.

The business was not in much better shape. We ended up selling all the assets of Arlanco and dissolving the corporation. Bankruptcy would have been an easy way out, but I chose to work and pay off the people we owed. I sold the machinery to Summit Timber, then went to work for them running the FMC Linkbelt excavator I had previously owned. I sold a piece of property to pay off a large note at the bank.

One day while running the excavator for Summit Timber, I had my most terrifying experience. I was knocking down some rock in a quarry so that it would be loaded into trucks without any danger of undermining the pit making it unsafe. I had climbed up high on the side of the pit on a very steep and narrow road I had to build as I went. I had reached the top and was in the process of knocking down all the loose rock I could reach while sitting on this little perch. Suddenly it seemed that the engine started running away. I decelerated the throttle, but it never slowed down. Then out of the clear blue sky, the wind started blowing and almost as suddenly a shadow came over me. Just as I had decided the end had come and the great evil spirit had come to get me, I looked up to see old Anthony and his helicopter hovering over me only five or six feet above the machine. What a relief. He landed nearby and said he just came to say good morning. I said "Good morning," but promised to get even someday when I could think of something mean enough.

In 1985, we borrowed money from the retirement fund I had accrued over the years and went back to Adam-ondi-Ahman for a reunion. It renewed a lot of the original great feelings of that sacred place.

In 1986, things started to look a little better for us. I had a good job and most of our financial obligations were arranged for, but it seemed like another kick in the head when we learned that Marie's cancer had returned and she had to have a mastectomy. I am so grateful for her attitude. What could have been another dark spot on my life was avoided by her positive attitude. She recovered quickly to be the same loving, caring person she had always been, depending completely upon the Lord.

It was a lot of fun working for Summit Timber. I loved the mountains and especially running the excavator. The pay was good and most of the road crew were great guys. My machine was smaller, 62000 lbs. and easy to move so, for this, reason I built a lot of landings and spur roads. Some of the bigger road jobs were Springsteen, North Gold, Donner, Daylight and many others. Bob Washburn, the road superintendent, was a nice guy to work for. I worked there until the spring of 1990. I was 69 years old.

One of our favorite experiences was in the later part of 1988 when Marie and I went to the east coast to see Kristy and Ellen and families. Kristy and Larry lived in Darien, Connecticut. We flew into White Plains, New York and Kristy picked us up there. It was Halloween night and she was dressed in her witch outfit. It was a fun time visiting with the kids. Larry commuted to New York City every day for his job. One day we met him there for lunch and we visited the Museum of Natural History, Central Park, Grand Central Station and we enjoyed the subways and train rides. One day, we drove up the coast and visited an old castle and a graveyard where some of our ancestors are buried. We went further north and visited an old restored whaling town where the sailing ships and docks and shops appear as they did in the 17th century. We thoroughly enjoyed our stay with them.

We flew on down to Tampa, Florida, and had an enjoyable time with Ellen and Marvin and family. Marvin was a new bishop and Ellen was in the Stake Young Women. They were very busy, but not too busy to show us a good time. One outstanding event was when we went on a twelve-mile canoe trip down the Alafia River. The river was low and very slow moving. It was like going through a wonderland of low hanging branches covered with Spanish moss. The mangroves and cypress grew all along the way. We saw lots of turtles and fish. They said there were alligators there, but we never saw any on this particular trip.

About half way along we decided to go ashore for a short rest. Ellen was in the front of Marv's canoe. When the bow of her boat ran up on the sand, she stepped out and Marv stood up just as Ellen went to pull the canoe up higher on the sandbar. The sudden jerk upset Marv and he did a backflip into the river, completely upside down and out of sight. That incident could have qualified for the best home video contest. We stayed in Florida a few days and thoroughly enjoyed the visit and their new home.

From there we flew on to Kansas City, rented a car and drove up to Adam-ondi-aham in Missouri. We went to their study class that night and although faces and names were different, the same spirit and comradery we had known five years before still existed. It was a real thrill to walk the grounds again and feel the aura of spiritual fragrance that emanates from that sacred land. We saw the wild turkeys and white tail deer and again visited the baptismal font where I had baptized my grandson, David Johnson, a few years before.

Before I quit working for Summit Timber, I became a lot better acquainted with Chad Erickson, the husband of Marie's daughter, Linda. I found him to be a very sharp engineer. We became involved in a land development project, he being a survey engineer and I an old road builder. We thought it would make a good partnership. We formed a corporation, Cedar Crest, and formally went into business. Our first project was a thirty plot in Mt. Vernon. We finished that project with the usual amount of success and hardships. Our next project was to be "Island Vista", an eighty-seven acre view property near Stanwood.

In 1990, one of the biggest events of a lifetime came when Marie and I left for a three week vacation. The high Point was the Cowley High School reunion.

Class Reunion
Left to right: Ester Stubbs, Evalou Marchant, Jared, Dudley Godfrey, Marjory Eyre, Leo Baird, Dorothy Baird, Irene Belue, Bernice Tucker

We loaded our camping gear into our new Dodge Dakota pickup and headed for Wyoming. We mostly drove straight through, stopping only to rest once in a while. We stopped at Margaret's, my brother Earl's widow, unloaded our gear and drove up in Little Mountain to the rim of Devil's Canyon. It was too late to go down into the canyon so we climbed in the back of the truck and went to bed. During the night, it started to rain. We were afraid the roads would be impassable by morning so we pulled back a few miles and waited until morning. The rain only grew worse so we left the mountain and drove back to Lovell.

We stopped at Zeller's to see Bessie and Clarence and found that John and Helen, Flora and Lowell, Ron and Alice and Leo and Dorothy were also there. It made quite a reunion. They took us on a tour through their candy factory. Up at Margaret's, we found that Katie and Thelma and Kurt had arrived. It was good to see everyone. That night we went up to Cowley to watch the basketball shootout and met a lot of our old Cowley friends. The next day they held the traditional Pioneer Day parade and a meeting in the church house.

In the afternoon all of the class of 1939 met at Esther Stubbs house and we were surprised to have fourteen of the original eighteen graduates there. It was sure fun to see everyone. Some I had not seen for fifty years. Saturday afternoon they held a beef barbecue. It was well planned and served. Then there was an open air program which was outstanding. The next day was Sunday. We went to church in Cowley where we met a lot more of our friends. All in all, there were over three thousand to the festivities at the Cowley High School Reunion.

Monday we went back to Devil's Canyon. The day was clear and fishing was good. We went down through the Hole in the Rock, and for the first time I found that my age was somewhat a handicap. It seemed harder to pull myself up the ropes with a creel full of fish. Not too many 69 year olds do that anymore.

Marie hiking and Devil's Canyon

The next day after visiting with Rex and Norma Eyre, we started towards home via the Big Horn Mountains. We spent the night at Big Baldy Campground and the next day fished in the Tongue River. Marie climbed a high mountain and took pictures for her exercise that day. We drove on to Sheridan, Wyoming; Custer's Battlefield; Billings, Montana; and spent the night in Red Lodge. It was our intention to go down into Deep Lake, but it was raining and foggy and after waiting half of the day, it didn't get any better so we drove on through Yellowstone Park and camped at Hebgen Lake. We stayed there until the next day and enjoyed the scenery and did a little fishing before leaving. We ended up on Ruby River and spent the night alongside the stream. We went to church in Twin Rivers and while there learned of some good fishing up on the Big Hole River so we could hardly wait to get there. We drove to Miners Lake and camped there for a few days. Fishing was good and we thoroughly enjoyed our stay there. The lake was full of grayling and brook trout.

Our next stop was at Spencer, Idaho. We heard of the opal mines and were determined to see if we could find some. We rented a shovel and hammer and I got a permit to dig. We spent four hours up on the mountain and learned a lot about mining opal. We left with two hundred pounds of rock, but probably not much opal. What we did get was pretty and I hope to do a lot of lapidary work. We also found some agate and jasper while on this trip. On the way home, we drove up through Libby, Montana, and found the grave of Marie's grandson, Scott Erickson. He died when he was only 24 hours old, but he had made a tremendous impression on Marie. We fished at Deep Lake and then drove on home via Leavenworth, Washington.

We had a little more work to do on the Cedar Crest subdivision to have it complete and had begun the acquisition of the Island Vista. We closed on that property October 15th and began clearing the lots and some of the roads. We have had an unusual amount of rain and the worst flood in recorded history. Because of this and the burning ban, we had to close down the construction part; but Chad had to do a lot of engineering and documentation.

July 1993

Left to right: Henry, Geneva Dickson; John, Helen Dickson; Jared, Marie Dickson; Katie Karlinsey, Bart Dickson; Kurt Karlinsey, Helen Dickson; Laura May, Bill Dickson; Gwyn Dickson

On December 14th, we left for a holiday vacation to California to visit our kids and grandchildren. We spent the first night in Olympia with Marie's niece and family, Keith and Terry Zaug. Then we went down to Lompoc to spend some time with Steve and Laurie Swallows and their family. We stayed there a week and enjoyed the grandchildren. We left there Sunday and got to Rancho Palos Verde in time to go to church with Ellen and Marvin and family.

Marie had a very difficult time the last two years of her life (1992-1993). Her cancer returned and was in her bones. It became more painful as it progressed. We spent a lot of time seeing doctors and taking treatments, radiation, etc. The biggest blow came when the cancer was discovered in the soft tissue of her brain and her diagnosis became terminal. The last six months I spent my entire time tending her and the house chores. I had some help from Hospice, and will be eternally grateful for her daughter, Linda Erickson, who came to help as much as possible.

I will not give a full account, but it will suffice to say that by tending to her every need, we formed a bond that will last through the eternities. I really loved her. December 30, 1993, Marie passed away, and for the second time I was left with a very vacant spot in my life. I am therefore thankful for a loving family and many friends who shared my grief. She was a tremendous person that touched the lives of all who knew her. I am most thankful for the knowledge of the gospel and a loving Father in Heaven who answers prayers and cares about his children.

Marie Spletter Dickson

1994 was quite an eventful year. We held our Jaredite family reunion out at the San Juan Islands. It was a good chance to get better acquainted with everyone.

# MARY

Jared and Mary

I became reacquainted with a longtime friend, Mary Alice (Marchant) Shurtleff. She was a wonderful, lovely lady. We were married December 2, 1994, in the Jordan River Temple in Salt Lake City, Utah.

Jared and Mary Alice

We both had a lot of hard and sad experiences. I suffered the loss in this life of two wonderful wives, but in the long run (eternities) it was not a loss at all, but very sad at the time. Mary Alice has had a life filled with both the good and the bad. She has raised a family that have stayed close and are well grounded spiritually. The bad part came a few years before we were married. Her husband left her for another woman and Mary had to fend for herself and go through the torment of being humiliated and the feeling of being cast out. How could anyone do such a thing to such a wonderful person as Mary?

From the time we were married, all things seemed to fall into place. It seems we both had the determination to make things work out. Our attitude, chemistry, and love for each other grew. I surely loved her. I learned that she had a crush on me in high school time many years before. I always admired her beauty and sense of humor and it seemed like a real match when both of our mates were gone. I am so grateful for events and circumstances that brought us together.

Lynn Dickson, Leo Baird and Jared

Our eighty-seven acre project at Island Vista never turned out so well with Chad Erickson. I became acquainted with Merle Ash who owned the Sand Technology Corp. and formed a partnership with him in Cedar Crest LLC. I was lucky to have him help me make the payments until we had the property ready for sale. It was a good experience with Merle.

In 1997, we sold a large portion of our property to Lery Corp. The proceeds completely paid off our indebtedness so Merle and I divided the property remaining between us. For my share, I took over a real estate contract on eleven acres and a promissory note which in 2003 and 2004 both were paid out and it ended my involvement with Merle Ash and the Island Vista property. During my time with Merle, I became well acquainted with Jeff Van Den Top who owned a lot of heavy equipment we rented to do the clearing and road building on the Island Vista project. He has become a very loyal and trusted friend. When with him I have a feeling of complete confidence. Although he is thirty years younger than I am, I can look to him for advice and guidance.

My long-time friend, Leo Baird, and I worked for Jeff on his property where he has brought a piece of no good land to the point of a near Garden of Eden proportions with several stocked trout ponds and grounds finished to a near gold course condition with miles of roads with landscaping and rockeries. We built bridges and docks, converted an old double-wide trailer into a state of art office building and assisted in developing a sports club complex with rifle range and shooting stands. He hosts a competitive shoot in each year where he invites two hundred of the best trap shooters in the nation to come and shoot.

Jared worked until he was 92 years old doing the work he called play.

On one of his shoot-in's it was a special occasion when he was married in an outdoor setting ceremony to his long-time friend Malinda

Malone. Leo and I and our wives were special guests. It was quite an honor.

On another occasion, Jeff hired Leo and I and my brother John to do one of his small projects in town. Leo and I were eighty years old and John was eighty-three. The superintendent of that job called us the cardiac gang. We did a fine job for him and really enjoyed it. Jeff gets quite a kick out of telling the rest of the crew how much experience we have had (about one hundred and eighty years combined).

Top row: John and Henry; bottom row: Katie, Jared and Thelma

Beth and Rob were married June 13, 1998. They were sealed in the Seattle Temple August 14, 2004. I was able to be one of the witnesses.

We were all saddened in April 2005 to learn that Jeff was diagnosed with pancreatic cancer. He was very ill and suggested he had only six weeks to live. They operated and felt sure he could recover.

Weeks of radiation and chemotherapy followed and in 2006 things looked good for him.

Jeff and I had a business deal that greatly benefited both of us. I bought some machinery from one of his companies and then rented it back to him on a lease purchase agreement. I got the depreciation write off plus monthly payments and interest. He got the write off for the lease payments. A win-win situation.

In Wyoming, I spent a lot of time with Earl's family. I can't say enough good things about them. I stayed at Marilyn's home and was especially pleased to see how she manages her home with seven daughters and no husband to support her. They find the time for family prayer, scripture study, music lessons, etc. What a wonderful job she is doing. Brian seems to be the patriarch now that Earl is gone. Everyone respects him and listens to his counsel. I feel they have left a legacy that will guide that family into the Celestial Kingdom.

Leo Baird, Helen and John
Bessie and Clarence Zeller

John, Leo, and Jared

Jeff, Leo Baird and his son, Wally

In review of my life thus far, I would like to comment on several things. I am grateful for the heritage I have and for the testimonies of those who have gone on before and for the strength I have gained from my older brothers and sisters. I could write volumes on the influence each one has had on my life. I just want everyone to know how much I appreciate them.

I know that I have been very blessed. I have reaped the rewards of living the gospel, probably more than I deserve. I have seen miracles performed on my behalf. I am thankful for the inner strength I have received at the time of the deaths of Elna, Marie and Mary Alice. No one has been of more strength to me than my own children and Marie's children and all our grandchildren. I love them all.

Jared in the Arlington parade

# Elna Lewis Dickson

I was born January 21, 1923, in my home at Cowley, Wyoming. I was the fourth of five children born to Edmund Elroy and Ellen Robertson Lewis. I was born of Wyoming pioneers. I lived in this same house until I left for college. I don't remember my preschool years, but with my sister, Veloy and brothers, Glenn and Elroy and later on Mark, I enjoyed life. We lived within a block of a cousin, Mary Alice Marchant. She was my same age and we were very close all through school.

I started school September 7, 1929 when I was six, and from the very first I loved school. Reading was my favorite subject and only found writing or penmanship difficult. My second-grade teacher, Mrs. Bunting, suggested that I skip that grade. My folks talked it over and then asked what I would like to do. I felt I had been with my friends for years and didn't want to go into a new grade with all new faces.

In the third grade, Norma Stevens was my teacher and her sister was in my class. I felt she showed favoritism. I came down with the mumps during this year and missed nearly six weeks of school. I had them on one side, and then when I thought I was through, I came down with them on the other side.

Every year the Saturday before Easter our family celebrated by going on an Easter hike or picnic. I came down with mumps for the second time on this Saturday morning. I was so disappointed to not get to go on the hike and watched my brothers and sister start out with their picnic sacks.

About this time in my life, my mother was sending me on an errand to my grandmothers, and I was looking back getting last minute instructions when I tripped over a broom and cut a huge gash in my left arm. My father was standing nearby talking to his Uncle Don Parkin, the county sheriff. They rushed me to Lovell to have it sewed up. I had a large scar for the rest of my life.

My favorite teacher during all my school years was my fifth-grade teacher, Miss Ella Yorgason. She brought some of her own personal books, a set of Nancy Drew books, and I loved them. She took me on hikes.

My grandfather Lewis lived all alone in a big, old house just through the block. My sister and cousins loved to go in his house and play with our Aunt's old clothes and shoes that were stored upstairs. She had lovely high button top shoes and hats with feathers. Another choice place to play especially on hot summer days was his ice house. Daddy would go in the winter time and chop blocks of ice which they would store in an ice house covered with sawdust. They would use this ice in the summer in our icebox refrigerators.

I was baptized by Miles Harston on June 7, 1931, in the old Harvey Pond. I was confirmed on the same day by my father.

At about this time in my life, my father decided I was old enough to work in the beet fields thinning beets on their Big Horn Valley ranch.

This has to be the worst way of making money. He paid us, but this didn't make me like it. Many times I was weeding or herding dad's sheep, or swimming in a nearby canal.

Every summer I looked forward to two special holidays. On the 4th of July, our Stake used to have Stake outings. This usually was a three day camping trip. Sometimes we didn't get to go for all three days, but we always went for one day. Another special day was the 24th of July celebration. The carnival would come to town, we would have a big parade, and Indians would come down and take part. My mother always made me a new dress for this special day.

I think the time I was the most frightened was when Glen, Veloy and I were home alone and these Indians rode up to our home. They wanted to put their horses in my father's pasture.

It was when I was eleven years old that a neighbor, Virginia Welch, and I put on a demonstration that won first in the county for 4-H. We were not allowed to go to state because I was not twelve years old. I also was first on a dress I made, and with the money that I won, I bought my first pair of roller skates. I was so proud of them.

Just before school started my parents would take us to Powell to the county fair or to Billings, Montana to the fair. This was looked forward to every year.

Our father bought us a riding horse called Colly. I loved to ride. I never used a saddle, but many times we enjoyed trips on horseback.

I'm afraid I was a handful in Primary and Sunday School. I went more to be with my friends. We made our teachers unhappy; never realizing what we were really missing.

In the sixth grade, we had a very lazy teacher and we didn't learn very much. Also, the school district ran out of money so school stopped in April. Our class went a couple of weeks long to school that the other grades because we were the oldest class in the building. It seemed odd to be the only ones attending in that huge building.

I felt I was really grown up when we moved to the high school building for the seventh grade. We had three different teachers. After coming in late from noon hour for several times and being warned, I and four of my friends were expelled. We could get back in school after we brought a note to school from our parents.

I dreaded going into eighth-grade. We had been told it was especially hard, but I enjoyed this year. Uncle Charles Marchant, Mary Alice's father, was the teacher. He used to get after me for spending so much of my time reading library books instead of studying. I especially remember him trying to teach art and how to draw. This was very hard for me.

This is the year I graduated from Primary and also they held an eighth-grade graduation ceremony. I was valedictorian of my class. My mother made me a green organdy dress that I thought was beautiful.

On September 8, 1937 I started as a freshman at Cowley High School. I now had my complete growth. The sophomores initiated us by making the girls wear hair braided and very short dresses. That year I took Home Economics, Algebra, English, Science, and Seminary. I enjoyed algebra, but hated science and got my lowest grade in it. I joined the Pep Squad and Home Ec clubs. My friends at this time were Geneva Stevens, Verda Stevens, Mary Alice Marchant and Flora Baird. The Tucker girls who had made up our group since first grade moved to California.

That summer I started to learn to play alto saxophone. I enjoyed belonging to the band, but never got too good; mostly because I found timing hard.

My sophomore year I joined Jr. Genealogy and that year we took a group to Canada on a temple excursion. This was a wonderful experience. It was during my ophomore year I first started dating Jared Dickson. On our first date, we went to see the show Gunga Din. It has always been a favorite.

I loved all the gym classes (baseball, basketball and volleyball). I also took speech and was in a couple of plays. I hated to miss school for any reason. I was voted student body vice president, senior class president, and Pep Club leader.

I dated Jared until he left for the Navy at the beginning of my senior year. I had a few dates with others, but boys were a means of transportation. My girlfriends were much more important to me at this time. On one date, Jared and his friend invited my girlfriend and me to go ice skating. We had never ice skated but had roller skated. We didn't want to look silly so several evenings immediately after school, we took ice skates and went out to my father's pond to practice. Jared and Jay were quite disgusted when they didn't have to hold us up all night and teach us to skate. We had a lovely time that summer. Jared, Jay Partridge, Rex Eyre, and all my girlfriends did a lot of things in a group.

Jared broke his ankle playing football that cramped his style. One night he didn't keep a date because he ran his tractor into the canal.

The night of my Baccalaureate my dad let me take our car and go to Lovell. One the way home we had followed a man who was going about twenty-five miles per hour. When I could pass him, I did. One of the girls reached over and honked the horn. He turned into me and caught my back fender. No other damage was done, but it was a new car and it spoiled my evening. I was again Valedictorian of my class and received a scholarship to the University of Wyoming.

That summer I worked for a short time at the cannery, and then went to the University of Wyoming in September. I roomed with a girl from Cowley, but I didn't know her very well. I worked doing housework part time to help with my expenses. I loved college life, but had a hard time with my accounting class. In November my mother got sick and they asked me to leave school and come home and take care of her.

Cowley looked bleak and desolate after Laramie. Because the war was going, I decided not to return to Laramie. Geneva Stevens and I went to Billings to a business college. We spent from January until June at college, and we really enjoyed each other and school. Geneva met her future husband and followed him to California so I decided not to return to Billings.

That fall I went to the L.D.S. Business College in Salt Lake City, Utah. I met and roomed with a girl from California. In October, her folks came to the conference and she was homesick. She talked me into going back to San Francisco for a week. My folks were very unhappy with me and told me I couldn't come home for Christmas.

I tried to find a job for the holidays but ended up taking a Civil Service job with Operating Engineers full-time. I've always been sorry I didn't finish my business training. I planned on finishing at night school, but kept too busy socially. Jared came to see me on his way home from leave, and I was elated. At Christmastime, I went to Tacoma to spend the holidays with him and his family and became engaged.

When Jared was sent overseas and things became quite dull, a girl I worked with at Redwood and I decided to join the Navy and do as much traveling as we could. Lila Fern was from Green River, Wyoming. After a few days at home, I joined her in Green River where we caught a train that took us to New York, where we entered Boot Camp. I loved it from the first. I received a sprain while there and was put on limited duty, but we enjoyed a couple of trips to New York. We visited the Empire State Building, the Statue of Liberty, Music Hall and other places.

Both Lila and I were sent to Cedar Falls, Iowa to yeoman school for a couple of months. We were really drilled and I felt if I could have stayed for a few more months, I would have mastered my shorthand. After two months, Lila Fern and I were both sent to San Francisco.

After a short leave, we arrived only to find there were no barracks available, but the Navy gave us sustenance and suggestions where we could stay. We finally ended up buying some people's furniture in order to get their apartment. Three Mormon girls and Lila, who was Catholic, moved into the apartment. We had a ball. The Navy provided trips to different resorts. I was close enough I could walk to work at the Federal Building. I enjoyed my boss and the six girls in the office. I worked in an office where we bought supplies for officer clubs overseas. I was able to check and tell where Jared's ship was at all times. One of the girls left to be married, but the three of us could afford the apartment and enjoyed more room.

The war came to a close and Jared was after me to get married. I wasn't sure what I wanted to do. I toyed with the idea of re-enlisting, but when Jared said now or never, I set the date for April 27. After being discharged from the Navy, I went home to get ready for the wedding.

Veloy was living at home and teaching in Cowley. She was a big help and made my wedding dress for me. One of Jared's brothers lent him his car and we drove to Salt Lake City. We stayed with his folks but were not married on the 27th because the temple wasn't open on Saturday. We had to wait until the 29th.

I was very disappointed in the temple ceremony. It seemed to take so long to get my endowments that I wasn't impressed at the actual marriage ceremony. His folks took us out for dinner, and we spent the evening at the Newhouse Hotel. We left the next morning on our honeymoon. We went up through Idaho and Jared insisted on us going to the Idaho Falls temple. I'm so glad he did because I enjoyed it this time.

We spent the summer taking care of my dad. We decided to leave and move out to Washington. I was very happy about this. I didn't want to live in Wyoming.

I wasn't very happy to find myself pregnant so soon, and it didn't help to have morning sickness all the time. We first moved into rough cabins. To heat the cabin, I would have to build a wood fire. I had quite a rough time doing this.

We found a nice home and I used the money I had saved during the Navy and bought furniture. We had our first nice home. Pregnancy has made me quite testy, and I had my feelings hurt quite easily. Our home also had a smaller house on the property. One night while alone I felt someone was out in the smaller house. When Jared came home, he found someone had been there. I was quite frightened.

I enjoyed these days of getting ready for our baby. Jared was working for his uncle. That winter the wind blew a great deal and it seemed the electricity was out a great deal. We often were forced to go to bed early to keep warm. Because of the war, we were unable to get a refrigerator. We had a difficult time keeping milk and vegetables crisp.

The night before Kathy was born, Jared was playing basketball, and they convinced me to try for a few baskets. About midnight I woke up feeling quite uncomfortable. About four o'clock in the morning we decided we had better go to Auburn where the hospital was. It was a nightmare. It was so foggy; we had to just creep along. When the doctor examined me he said I had a long way to go. I was so angry with him. I felt I could never last. I swore I would never have another baby. Jared went home and was not there when Kathy was born because I had her faster than the doctors thought I would.

The nicest feeling I felt was to feel flat again. When they wheeled me back to my room, I was so pleased with myself; I had smiles all over. I had been determined I was having a boy, but one look at our new baby girl and we would not trade her.

At this time, I missed my mother more than at any time. I had never been around babies. Poor Kathy was raised by a book Veloy had sent me. I put her on a schedule suggested by the book, and I did not vary by as much as five minutes. Thinking back, she was a very good baby.

We went to Seattle and came home with a new car. We were so proud of it. Everything seemed to be going our way. One night Jared's dad called and convinced him his place was back home with Earl and Henry. I was just sick, but we let our house go back, and we packed up all our furniture and headed for Wyoming.

We bought a small, one bedroom home and Jared went to work for his brothers. That was some winter. The gas made the doors swell and they would not shut tight. I found I was starving Kathy, and I had to put her on formula. I was called to work in the M.I.A. as a counselor, and though I tried, I felt I didn't add too much. It was a learning experience.

We were living here while Linda was born. She was a beautiful baby. Kathy was a very mischievous two-year old. During this time, she put things in the broiler. I would light the broiler to find a singed cat, burnt overalls, etc. I used to fill tubs to rinse my clothes. One day she picked up her dad's muddy boots and threw one in each of the tubs. I had the tubs to empty and fill by hand again.

Jared built us two more bedrooms. I was called to work in Stake Primary as a Lark teacher. I really enjoyed working in this calling. When I found I was pregnant again, I was really unhappy and I'm afraid I gave Jared a bad time. I was thinking of asking to be released from the Stake Primary, but when they set me apart, President Brown seemed

*This was all the paperwork I had on Elna except her obituary which I've added here:*

Elna was a born leader, and she proved to be so at every undertaking. She has served extensively in many church organizations on ward and stake levels and was serving as stake Educational counselor in the Relief Society at the time of her death.

Made in the USA
San Bernardino,
CA